THE STORY OF THE WORLD'S OLDEST PROFESSION

Prostitution in the Ancient, Medieval and Modern Worlds

I0026962

by

Joseph McCabe

THE BOOK TREE
San Diego, California

ISBN 978-1-58509-366-3

Cover Image
© frankie's

Cover Layout
Mike Sparrow

Published by
The Book Tree
P O Box 16476
San Diego, CA 92176
www.thebooktree.com

We provide fascinating and educational products to help awaken the public to new ideas and
information that would not be available otherwise.
Call 1 (800) 700-8733 for our *FREE BOOK TREE CATALOG*.

CONTENTS

PREFACE

Since the title plainly tells the aim and contents of this work, very few introductory words are needed. I would merely apprise the reader that it is not simply a collection of sketches of the picturesque life of prostitutes in different ages and environments. It is, as far as the historical evidence is available—and the bibliography at the close will show through what a range of literature I have sought it—a complete study, from the historical viewpoint, of an aspect of sex-life which is of exceptional interest yet very scantily treated in our literature. The only manual in the English language, W. W. Sanger's *History of Prostitution*, is not merely now rare, but it is really a study of modern prostitution with a very imperfect and not very accurate historical introduction, chiefly borrowed from Dufour's ancient work. Mr. Havelock Ellis has only a few pages, not wholly accurate, on the historical interest in the sixth volume of his *Psychology of Sex*, and Professor Westermarck is as unsatisfactory in his *Origin and Development of the Moral Ideas*. It will be noticed that articles in the best works of reference find it almost impossible to recommend to the reader any available literature on the subject. I have here collected the facts from a large collection of general historical works and local studies, and I offer my readers a unique and complete study of one of the most interesting aspects of sexual behavior.

THE STORY OF THE WORLD'S OLDEST PROFESSION

CHAPTER I

PROSTITUTION AMONGST SAVAGES

HE northwestern groups of the beautiful and languorous islands of the Pacific are occupied by a black folk, the Melanesians, who remain at one of the lowest levels of existing humanity. In spite of the streams of higher races which have passed over the region and in some ways affected their life, they in the main have simple practices which are only one degree higher than those of the blacks of Australia. Yet amongst their primitive institutions we almost invariably find prostitution. In some islands one encounters it only in the rudimentary form that the unmarried girl accepts presents of ornaments or food for the bestowal of her favors; though, since there is naturally no coinage and all services are thus paid in kind, there is in this little difference from formal prostitution. In a few islands, in which the blacks demand that a girl shall remain a virgin until she marries. it is the transgressor of the tribal rule who, if she becomes pregnant, is compelled to become a common harlot. But in most of the islands, where the general attitude toward sex is so naturalistic that parents will look fondly on while their nude boys and girls of six and seven lie in the dust before them and play at marriage, there is an extensive and recognized system of prostitution. Sometimes the unmarried girls or the widows formally, and not at all furtively, trade with their bodies. In other places men buy the daughters of impoverished or greedy neighbors and make money by what one may call the black slave traffic. These girls are no more respected than the poorer harlots of civilized lands, but there is in some of the larger islands a class of women who are almost privileged members of the community. They belong to the chief and live in huts near his house, and to these the young men repair openly. Their earnings go to the chief; and, since he is generally also the primitive priest or sacrificer, we here have, though no religious significance is attached to the sex-act itself, the beginning of that close association of temple and brothel which provides one of the most singular chapters in the history of prostitution.

Since we thus find a system of prostitution developed at one of the lowest and most primitive levels of human life, we need not quarrel with the statement that it is "the oldest profession in the world": certainly, the oldest paid profession of the female sex. Nor must we for a moment suppose that the sensual conditions of life in tropical islands—the abundant food, the easy indolence, the habitual nudity of the alluring forms of the young women—have here forced the pace of sexual growth. In the bleak and cold conditions of the far north, amongst many of the peoples which, from Canada to Kamchatka, struggle for a living on the fringe of the great ice-sheet, we find a different but extensive development of the trade. The earliest travelers to Greenland and some other arctic regions found female prostitution already prevalent amongst the Eskimo as an aboriginal practice. Amongst the natives of arctic or semi-arctic Asia, on the other hand, where the proportion of women is smaller, we find a great deal of male prostitution. Parents of a boy who approaches the feminine type in appearance often dress and rear him as a girl, and they sell him in his early teens to some wealthier native. The shamans or priest-wizards, who frequently wear female dress, add to their store of furs or food by occasionally prostituting themselves.

In every climate, at every grade of culture above that of the Australian black, we find, contrary to the statement of Mr. Havelock Ellis, primitive peoples developing some form of prostitution. And I need not remind my readers that this is no relic of an original promiscuity. On the contrary, the really lowest representatives of the human family live in strict monogamy and have nothing that approaches prostitution or promiscuous intercourse; and this seems, as I have elsewhere explained, to have been the general condition of the race during the millions of years of advance beyond the purely animal stage. Prostitution appears with social life, and it is an inevitable outcome of its psychic and economic conditions. The lowest peoples live at the most in groups of three or four related families. Few of the males that are born reach maturity, and these few leave the small colony at maturity and pair elsewhere. The three or four men who remain in the community are now tempted to find a monotony in monogamy since the three or four mature females are all of the same ungainly type and all paired.

Anything of the nature of prostitution is inconceivable in these extremely small social groups. The impulse toward it arises in the larger social groups, where the male is stimulated by the number and variety of the women, and young unmarried males multiply. We might expect to find it amongst the merry and free-living Bushmen of South Africa, especially as they have considerable artistic taste, but the social group is still small, and the sex-adventures of each member are watched with a cynical gaiety. The only approach to prostitution is that wives are often attracted from their husbands by men who can provide more and richer food.

Among the Australian blacks, on the other hand, no man who is acquainted with their peculiar sex-behavior will expect to find prostitutes. The older men of a settlement are despotic tyrants, and they use their mystic power to secure for themselves all the desirable young women. The mature youth, who is at once married by the tribal authorities on a very complicated scheme of relationship, must wait years before he can enjoy his bride. To remove from him the temptation to intrigue or elope, which would bring a death-sentence upon him, his elders provide him with a boy or an elderly woman. The mature girls are appropriated by the men of the ruling council. So the wise ancestors are supposed to have decreed, and their laws are truculently enforced by the men in power. There is a very great diversity in the black world of Australia, but this was the common arrangement before the coming of the whites, who, of course, soon initiated the native women to prostitution.

In every branch of the race above this level, though naturally not in every section of it, there has been a development of prostitution in some form. We do not expect a consistent development, since the savage attitude toward sex varies amazingly, and it is often so lenient that there is no need of professional women. In a tribe where the unmarried girls are free to do as they please, as they are in probably the majority of savage tribes, the unmarried or more robust males hardly require any other satisfaction; especially if, as is common, they are polygamous. Sir Harry Johnston, who has an unrivaled knowledge of British Central Africa, and who is rather disposed to puritanism than to any over-emphasis on sex, tells us that in the whole of that vast area "scarcely any girl remains a virgin after about five years of age." One may read in Professor Westermarck's ample collection of facts that this remarkable freedom with young girls, though sometimes only after their seventh or eighth year, is found in many other parts of Africa (including Madagascar), and in Melanesia, Polynesia, Indonesia (including the Philippine Islands), and northeastern Asia. Amongst other tribes a girl who has been carefully watched until marriage becomes common property for a time after that ceremony. Polygamy also helps to meet the growing demand of the male for variety, and we must further take into account the seasonal orgies, when complete promiscuity is often permitted, and the broad license of weddings and other feasts.

In spite of these alleviations of the male impulse we find almost everywhere a tendency to create a class of prostitutes. Africa, in spite of the general polygamy and use of the unmarried girls, provides a number of instances which illustrate the development. Emin Pasha, another high authority on Central Africa, tells us that he found prostitution everywhere, but that it is "officially sanctioned" only in the country of the Wanyoro (Uganda). There the king provides his wives with a large number of female servants, and he encourages these in the practice of prostitution. The only service they render to himself—he has a very spacious harem—is the dance, and he does not share their earnings. They appeal to him when a man is ungenerous or unjust in paying them for their services, and he permits them to hire themselves at any time for four or five days to a native. If they have female children while they are in the king's service, these are compelled to follow the profession of the mother, but the women often become relatively rich and may marry.

Emin Pasha is not correct in thinking that this is the only, or even the most conspicuous, instance of recognized prostitution in Africa. Winwood Reade tells us in his Savage Africa that he found a more advanced system in Northern Guinea. There the prostitutes belong to what one may call the municipal authorities of the native towns, and they are reared and trained for the purpose. They live apart from the other women and wear special dress or carry bells. This, however, does not mean that they are regarded with contempt. It seems that it "is the custom for rich negro ladies, on their death-beds, to buy female slaves and present them to the public." The more they provide, Reade says, the richer will be their reward in the black heaven. The earnings of the women go to the authorities, who provide them with food, clothing, and huts. They are so sought that the first act of the authorities in time of trouble is to close the brothels, when the bachelors quickly submit; and it is said that the married natives also, to protect their wives, implore the governors to raise the embargo.

In this richly varied world of African life we find also the beginning of sacred prostitution. Major Ellis gives several instances in his authoritative works on the natives of the western coast. On the Slave Coast, he says, "there is in every town at least one institution in which the best-looking girls, between ten or twelve, are received." They remain in these nunneries three years, learning the chants and dances which are required in the worship of the gods and submitting to the embraces of the black priests. At the end of the period of training they become formal temple-prostitutes. By the rules they ought to confine their services to male worshippers, but they serve, without reproach, as general prostitutes to the community. They are the wives of the god and as such have much prestige. A different kind of temple-prostitution is found among the natives of the Gold Coast. Here there is a phallic deity, Legba, who is frankly regarded, not as the solemn spirit that fertilizes cattle and crops, but as the smiling god of the orgasm and the erotic dream. His nude image, with enormous phallus, which he contemplates with savage joy, confronts even the children everywhere. The priestesses are his wives, and on the night of the special festivals they retire to the forest with the men, whom the priests have stimulated with powerful aphrodisiacs in the native beer. They are women of insatiable sex-impulses, and they are granted complete license at all times. They choose—it is a sort of royal command—their own lovers, and one may see a fat priestess at times walking in public with half a dozen of them. As priestesses of a simple god of sexual love, the more "debauched" they are, from the European visitor's viewpoint, the more effective is their ministry.

It is unnecessary to tell the variations of the trade in every part of the Black Continent. When so expert a writer as Emin Pasha tells us that there is prostitution everywhere, we may at least conclude that it is a general custom, and that is enough for my present purpose. There is just as great a variety of sexual conduct and of ideas about sex in the native world of America, and at least among the lower tribes there is, or was, a good deal of prostitution. The Omahas had a recognized caste of harlots and permitted extra-matrimonial intercourse only with these. If a girl or woman went about alone, she was liable to be regarded as one of the minchedas and addressed accordingly. In their highest representatives, the Mayans and Peruvians, the American Indians had strict ideas of sexual virtue, but they admitted public prostitution. Amongst the lower tribes of South America there was a very elaborate and candid system of prostitution. In parts of Brazil there was, as in northern Asia, a practice of dressing and rearing the more handsome boys as girls, and we may note again how little difference it makes in regard to sex whether a tribe is in the frozen north or in voluptuous tropical forests, with abundance of food and women. Amongst these Brazilian tribes there was also the complementary custom, that the more virile girls were allowed to live, work, and fight as males and to take "wives." Some of the eastern Eskimo and a few of the African peoples had the same practice. An element of prostitution often appeared, as the women, who always avoided males, sometimes had to bribe other women or girls to have relations with them.

In the Asiatic continent there was an even greater diversity. It is said in excuse of the male prostitutes of the northern peoples that they thus sought to restrict the growth of population in regions where food is so scarce that the aged, and sometimes batches of adults, had to be killed. But in the fertile islands of the Indian Ocean the practice was just as rife. Amongst the Dyaks of Borneo there was a recognized caste of men, the basir, who dressed as women and were often ceremonially married to men. In the license of festivals they prostituted themselves to all. Some tribes despised them, but others regarded them as normal members of the community. It was the same in parts of Sumatra and other islands. A corresponding caste of effeminate men in Madagascar, the tsecats, used to pay men to sleep with them. And it need hardly be said that we find the same practice in Tahiti and other Polynesian islands. There are few varieties of sexual behavior with which the Polynesians were not acquainted.

On the other hand, what is called in ethical literature polyandry is often merely a variety of prostitution. It was at one time particularly prevalent in southern Asia, especially round the fringes of India, and it must at first have been the common form of prostitution over the greater part of southern Asia. Possibly there was at one time a scarcity of women which led to the practice, but it usually gives the woman a higher position in the community, and it has been retained by very many peoples. Generally the woman formally marries a group of brothers (among the Todas) or is understood to be married to her husband's uncles and nephews as well as his brothers (Bhils, etc.). In other mountainous regions between India and Thibet, and in Thibet, several brothers live together with their wives, and there is no exclusiveness about their sexual relations. Except in Thibet the women are virile and independent, and they often choose lovers outside the family circle; when the element of prostitution is very apt to appear. In Cochin and Malabar a girl is first married to a youth who does not thereby acquire the rights of a husband. She then "marries"— in effect, she is a prostitute— a number of men and receives payment from all for her services. The Jats of Baluchistan and some others, even in India, make money by the prostitution of their wives. In short, all over southern Asia we find amorous arrangements which are thinly disguised or open forms of prostitution. Of India itself, where the wives are, as a rule, strictly controlled, we will speak later. It is a classic land of prostitution. Apart from that country, the peculiarity of Asiatic ideas is that a sort of ethical color is given to the woman's conduct by assuming that the husband's relatives share his conjugal privileges.

It may be thought that the Aryans introduced stricter ideas into Asia, but there is much evidence that the pre-civilized Aryans of Europe generally had not at all puritanical ideas. There are today, east of the Carpathian Mountains, parts of Slav Europe where it is held that a man has the right of intercourse with his son's wives, and there are many districts, from the Balkans to Ireland, where quaint features of the wedding festivities suggest that at one time the bride was for a time common to the guests. But over at least half of pre-civilized Europe chastity was not expected in a bride, and as the tribes lived in small pastoral communities, we should expect to find very little prostitution; certainly nothing in the nature of an institution.

So little real historical work has been expended on the subject of prostitution that we must regard these as a few instances which have been rather casually gleaned from the works of travelers. They are, however, sufficient to show that from the time when men first began to live in groups of a hundred or more, women—and before long men—began the trade of prostitution. The causes also are clear enough. In the case of widows or rejected wives we may recognize economic pressure, but it is a very subsidiary cause. In other cases the girl is virtually in the position of a slave, and her mode of life is dictated. But this in all cases clearly agrees with her inclination, and we may say that from the start the general explanation of both occasional and permanent or professional prostitution is that girls or women regard it as, in plain modern speech, an easy way of making money. With the progress of social life marriage is postponed, especially where the bride must be bought, and there are years of impatient bachelordom; while, on the other hand, even the married men are stimulated to seek variety by the sight of so many unattached young women in the community. The new need is met, as we saw, in many different ways—polygamy, orgies, freedom to the unmarried, prostitution of priestesses, etc.— but a professional caste appears as naturally as in the case of any other demand, and chiefs and priests begin at an early date to organize the trade for their own profit.

CHAPTER II

IN THE ANCIENT CIVILIZATIONS

ONE can understand why it is difficult to trace the development of prostitution in pre-civilized times, because travelers in savage lands usually take note only of the phenomena which are unfamiliar to them, such as male prostitution and polyandry. But it is just as difficult to follow the evolution of the profession in the earlier part of the civilized period. In the case of Egypt we have now a most vivid and detailed knowledge of the life of all classes from the earliest historical times, yet all that we positively know about prostitution in that country, until the Greek historian Herodotus visits it in the fifth century B. C., can be told in a few lines. For the Babylonians we have even less information until we come to the same Greek historian and his statements about sacred prostitution. About the Cretans we know nothing in this respect, for we cannot read what little literature of theirs we have. It would astonish many pious folk to know that, as far as positive documents go, we have almost no undisputed evidence of prostitution amongst these wicked nations, and that the Hebrews are the first people of antiquity to exhibit it to us on a large scale. Even when we adopt the new chronology of the Old Testament, it remains the oldest document in the world about prostitution, and, until the Greeks began to describe their neighbors, the Bible is the richest account of ancient prostitution that we have.

Therefore I will not here attempt to strain or expand the scanty evidence but will merely, for the older nations, discuss a few points in which some of our modern writers mislead their readers. In the case of Egypt the few references to prostitutes merely justify us in assuming that, since simple fornication, or intercourse with unmarried women, was apparently not condemned by the Egyptian code, brothels were probably as numerous as in any other advanced civilizations, ancient or modern. Sanger, who is very uncritical in his early chapters, gives the gay life of the city of Naucratis as an example of the sex-life of the Egyptians. But Naucratis, the predecessor of Alexandria at the mouth of the Nile, was a Greek city, or commercial settlement, with entirely Greek manners and institutions. The only positive evidence is that certain of the moral treatises or essays which we find in the tombs warn youths to beware of the "strange women," or women who have left their husbands or been abandoned by them and travel from city to city; and that in one tomb some cynical merchant or official has had very salacious pictures buried with him. This may seem to confirm the old theory, that the Egyptians were a particularly solemn and religious people, with more regard for chastity than other ancient nations, but I showed in my **Story of Human Morals** that the evidence gathered in the last thirty years has discredited this view. The Egyptians were as merry and sensual, as fond of beer and wine and festivals, as the Greeks. Their love-songs (some of which are preserved in the **Song of Solomon** in the Bible) were very candid and naturalistic. Their stories very frequently, and sometimes cynically, turned on sex. Herodotus reproduces one about a blind king who was told that he would recover his sight if he washed his eyes in the water of a faithful wife, and he used the water of his own wives and many others without obtaining any result. One absurd story was that Cheops had got the whole cost of building his great pyramid by prostituting his daughters. Another story, which Maspero has translated in his **Popular Tales of Ancient Egypt**, runs that a king, in the hope of catching an audacious thief, bade his daughter prostitute herself to all comers, stipulating that each should confess

to her the boldest deed of his life. That Egyptian kings prostituted
their daughters is monstrously incorrect, but the popularity of such
stories and songs indicates very liberal sentiments about sex. We
know further that in official documents the workers are often described as having "women" instead of wives, and that there was a
phallic gaiety in the villages at the festival of Osiris (and a few
other gods) as naive as in the villages of the Gold Coast. The
women boisterously carried about an image of Osiris with a phallus,
worked by cords, as large as the body.

We may therefore assume that the harlot was as familiar a
figure in Egyptian towns as in modern towns. It is a more difficult
and disputed question whether there was sacred prostitution in the
temples. The writer on the subject in the Encyclopaedia of Religion
and Ethics is "certain" that there was. He has a peculiar method
of proving it. From Herodotus he takes the absurd legend that
Cheops (or Khufu) built his pyramid out of the proceeds of the
prostitution of his daughters, and we are asked to think that they
were probably temple-prostitutes! Another story in Herodotus—
and here he speaks as eye-witness—is that on a certain annual festival boat-loads of men and women, with musicians, sailing along
the Nile, used to stop opposite a town and exchange abusive epithets
with the women of the town, the boat-women in the end lifting their
robes and exposing their persons. I suggest, from observation in
many lands, that in contempt the half-drunken ladies exposed the
rear of their persons, but Professor Burton is sure that they were
priestesses performing a phallic rite! He has not noticed, apparently, that Herodotus expressly says that there were no temple-
prostitutes in Egypt. "Nearly all peoples," he says, "except the
Egyptians and the Greeks have intercourse with women in sacred
places." The only impressive evidence is that the Greek geographer
Strabo, who traveled in Egypt, says of the Thebans of his time:

> To Jupiter [Ammon], whom they especially venerate,
> they dedicate a virgin of high birth and great beauty. She
> has intercourse with any she wishes, like a courtesan, until
> her natural purification is accomplished.

In other words, ladies, or some ladies, of high birth prostituted
themselves in the great temple of Thebes during the month before
they married. It is puzzling, especially as, at an earlier date,
Herodotus had found a community of chaste nuns attached to this
temple. Many authorities reject Strabo's story. Apart from it we
have only an inscription of King Rameses III to the effect that he
dedicated to the service of the temple all the women of a conquered
people, and that certain paintings on the wall of a temple at Medinet
Abu seem to be "harem scenes." As women served innocently in
the temples all over Egypt, this is not decisive. Possibly the solution of it all is that temple-practices from Syria were introduced
here and there after the time of Herodotus, just as ascetic ideas of
celibate communities of both men and women were introduced.

This seems natural enough when we reflect on the kind of life
which the Greeks introduced into Egypt. As early as the seventh

century, apparently, the Greek colonials founded the city of Naucratis at the mouth of the Nile, and there, free from the fanatical control of their own cities, they established a life of remarkable gaiety and opulence. The austere Herodotus himself devotes two pages to the most famous courtesan of this city, Rhodopis (the Rosy-Cheeked); and she is the lady whom Sappho fiercely assails for emptying her brother's treasury. She was a beautiful Thracian slave whom Sappho's brother found in a brothel at Naucratis, and he purchased her liberty. She became famous throughout civilization and acquired such wealth that legend credited her with the building of a pyramid. She is the first of the great courtesans of the Greek world, who were honored by all, and her life clearly shows that before the year 600 B. C. a higher type of prostitution flourished in the Greco-Egyptian city. Its character we shall see in the fourth chapter; and to that chapter we may defer an account of the way in which the Ptolemies encouraged the profession in Alexandria. They raised statues in the public squares to their favorite courtesans. Before the beginning of the Christian Era Alexandria abounded in prostitutes of every type. Those of the common type sat at their windows, dressed in saffron robes and heavily painted, singing love-songs to attract further attention. A Roman soldier complained that one seized his arm in the street and, when he refused to go with her, spat in his face. The Roman officers and soldiers were not usually so delicate, and they themselves founded brothels in garrison towns all over Egypt.

Babylonian literature can be almost divided into religious and commercial, and it contains no references to either courtesans or brothels. We do not, however, need the invectives of the Hebrew prophets to suggest to us that there was in the cities of Mesopotamia a normal amount of prostitution. The Babylonian moral code no more forbade simple fornication than did the Egyptian. But we know nothing about this aspect of Babylonian life until the time of Alexander the Great. It is enough that, as I have proved in several works, we have not the least ground in positive evidence to say that the Babylonians were sexually looser than others, and we have some ground in the terrible sexual clauses of their criminal code and in their religious ideas to suppose that they were not.

Probably all readers of this book will have seen my earlier works (Little Blue Book No. 1076, Morality in Ancient Babylon, and Vol. II of the Story of Human Morals) and will know what to think of the very common statement, based upon Herodotus, that all the women of Babylon had to prostitute themselves in the temple before they could marry. The story is ridiculous in detail, as it represents that a great crowd of women waited in the court of the temple for some stranger to choose them, and that the less-favored of them had to wait for years. There would not be an average of twenty marriages a day in Babylon, and there would be at all times thousands of male "strangers" (sailors, merchants, provincial workers and officials, etc.) in the city. A virgin, however homely, who could in such a city be hired for the smallest piece of silver (less than a dime) would not wait an hour. We now know, in fact, that the women of Babylon generally had no such duty, for the marriage tablets habitually state that the bride is a virgin; so that both Herodotus and Strabo are wrong. Burton (Encyclopaedia of Religion and Ethics), who finds sacred prostitution everywhere, and others maintain that certain classes of women, and even men, who are mentioned in the Hammurabi Code as servants of the temples were prostitutes. This is denied by other experts and is very uncertain. Yet I quoted in the Story of Human Morals (II, 39) a moral poem in which a youth is warned against marrying three types of women, "the strange woman whose lovers are many" (clearly a prostitute), "the maiden of Ishtar," and "the woman servant of the temple," as equally "set upon the path of the stranger." I conclude, as I did from the first, that, while the story told by Herodotus is ridiculously untrue, there may have been a few old temples of Ishtar with sacred prostitutes. Ishtar was an ethical goddess in the classic period of Babylon.

It is possible that these old phallic temples—there seems to be a reference to one at Erech in the ancient Epic of Gilgamesh—received a new vitality when, in the first millennium before Christ, the old civilizations weakened, and the influence of phallic Asia Minor spread over the world. Certainly Alexander the Great found the city of Babylon much more free and sensual than it seems to have been in earlier times. An officer who was in his army, Quintus Curtius, has left us a remarkable description of the social condition. The men were, he says, very drunken, and they were very ready to prostitute their wives to the Greek soldiers. Women and girls of the higher class, he says, sat at table with courtesans, and they drank so much that presently they threw off their outer garments and in the end even their underclothes. Here a thoroughly hostile visitor—he was disgusted at Alexander's lingering with his courtesans in the city—may be repeating gossipy exaggerations, but we do know that about this time a fashion of greater freedom had spread throughout the civilized world, as we shall see later.

It was the Persians who had brought the new spirit to Babylon, but they had merely adopted the free practices of Asia Minor and the Greeks, which we shall see presently. It is in the Persian sacred book, the Avesta, that we find the first moral fulmination against the prostitute. "Any woman," it says, "that has given up her body to two men in one day is sooner to be killed than a wolf, a lion, or a snake." How this Zoroastrian religion gave the world the first explicit doctrine of chastity—on the crude ground that the supreme devil had created all matter and therefore the body—and in time led to the embodiment of that doctrine in Mithraism, some Greek philosophies, and Christianity, I have explained elsewhere. But in the century or two of their first spell of world-power the Persians themselves took very little notice of it. Until the time of Cyrus the Great they had been a rude pastoral folk of very simple habits. After the conquests of Cyrus they changed as rapidly as does the farmer's son who makes a fortune in New York or Chicago. Darius, who confronted Alexander, is said to have always had three hundred and fifty elegant courtesans in camp with him. We are told that when Alexander beat him, his officers found in the deserted royal camp three hundred and twenty-nine singing and dancing girls of the harem, two hundred and seventy cooks, seventy "philterers of wine," and forty perfumers. At banquets in the Persian cities, the same Greek writer tells us, it had become customary for the girls and women, in spite of the thunders of the Avesta about the Day of Judgment, to sit in transparent silks or with no other covering than flowers. Prostitution had, naturally, reached the same height as in all other cities of the few centuries before Christ.

In other words, ascetic religion was at first heavily defeated when it set out to conquer the old freedom, but we shall understand this better when we have seen the amorous life of Asia Minor and Greece which seduced the older nations. Here it remains only to say a few words about the rich development of prostitution in Judaea which is so amusingly taught to the children of our puritanical world from the Bible.

The difficulty of extracting social history from the Old Testament is that, while we now know that no single book or chapter was written before the year 1000, as the Hebrews had no written language, we cannot date any of the statements about Hebrew life until long after that time. Modern writers who still repeat that Moses permitted prostitution, provided the women were foreigners, and that prostitution was a recognized institution (Genesis, 38:14) long before the time of Moses, betray a strange ignorance of Hebrew literature. The crude story of Tamar dressing as a prostitute in order to have intercourse with her father-in-law, which would be denounced as a piece of unspeakable oriental depravity if it were in the Arabian Nights, clearly belongs to a time when, at least after 1200 B. C., the Hebrews were settled in Palestine. It probably depicts life in Palestine long after 1000 B. C., when the towns were large and rich enough to have colonies of harlots sitting in booths or tents beside the roads, to whom quite respectable Hebrews repaired without a blush. Legend has it that the amorous Solomon hospitably admitted them within the cities. The most that we can deduct from all these statements of the Pentateuch is that there was a tradition in Judaea that during the first few centuries of the settlement in the country native girls were forbidden to become prostitutes, and foreign women (from Moab, Edom, etc.) were suffered to live in brightly colored tents, with a show of cheap merchandise, outside the towns; and that by about the year 1000 B. C. the restrictions were removed, and Jerusalem had its harlots' quarter like every other Syrian town.

There are, however, many scholars who think that Tamar, in order to win her father-in-law, Judah, dressed herself as a temple-prostitute, so that from the start the Hebrews shared that institution with their neighbors. The details of the story do not seem to me to point in the least to temple-prostitution—"she covered her with a veil, and wrapped herself, and sat in an open place"—nor could we, in that case, understand why only foreign women were used in the cult. I suggest that the years of wandering pastoral life had given no opportunity for the development of prostitution and, when the Hebrews settled in Palestine, they forbade their daughters to take up the trade and, as they made wealth, used the Syrian women. But the example of their Syrian neighbors, whose superior ways they soon began to imitate, led them very early to adopt phallic cults. One of the oldest books of the Old Testament is the prophecy of Hosea, and in the fourth chapter the truculent anti-clerical represents the whole nation as addicted to phallic worship. The priests "sacrifice with harlots" "upon the tops of mountains" and under trees. In the light of later texts this clearly means that there is a cult of a goddess of fertility, and that her priestesses are sacred prostitutes.

Hosea was probably written about the middle of the eighth century, when we first have sound historical evidence that the Hebrews have become civilized. As part of that process, they had clearly adopted the goddess of love of their Syrian neighbors, with the full apparatus of phallic emblems and consecrated prostitutes, probably both male and female. The references to the same system in Deuteronomy and I Kings (which puts "Sodomites in the land" in the tenth century) are of very late date and unreliable, but the circumstantial story of a reform of the cult in the year 622 B. C., by King Josiah (II Kings, XXII) is accepted by all scholars. It shows that the worship of Jahveh had almost ceased to exist, and the whole of the people and priests followed the Syrian religions. Under the very shadow of the temple, which housed a large phallic emblem (stupidly translated "grove" in the English Bible), were "the houses of the Sodomites"; or the rooms of the effeminately dressed and highly painted ministers of the love-goddess who prostituted themselves to all comers. In the temple itself, or probably in rooms round its courtyard, were the women who "wove hangings for the grove"; that is to say, the consecrated harlots who embroidered the rich coverings of the phallic emblems and earned money by prostitution for the temple. At the gates of the city, in the woods outside it, on the tops of the hills, and in all the cities of Judaea were other temples of love with sacred prostitutes. It is, apart from a work of the Greek writer Lucian, the most complete description of a system of sacred prostitution in all literature.

This system had, with a few temporary attempts at reform, lasted from the beginning of Hebrew civilization, as far as we have reliable documents, and the Old Testament says that after the death of King Josiah the Hebrews reverted to it. Apparently it continued until the Babylonians ruined and impoverished the land, and upon the ruins the new priests raised the structure of worship that they put into the mouth of Moses. From the fact that they took the trouble to make him forbid sacred prostitution, it seems that it still continued. The system was still, or again, established in the second century, for the temple is said in the books of the Maccabees to be a brothel, "full of those who sin with harlots." It seems that the fierce national struggle then concentrated the people on the worship of Jahveh, and sacred prostitution disappeared. But the ladies did not retire far. From the stories of the Talmud we learn that a special market-place in Jerusalem was occupied by them, since the book boasts of the virtue of a shoemaker who lived there and worked for the women yet never lifted his eyes to them. Other stories tell of Jews who have temporary wives when they travel, and one says that in the first century A. D. adultery had become so common that the old law had to be suspended. The New Testament, if we care to trust its stories, confirms that Judaea had still as plentiful a supply of prostitutes as any other civilized country. In short—the reader may care to put this paradox to his religious neighbors—those scarlet sins of ancient Babylon on which they dwell so fondly have no firm support whatever in the ample Babylonian literature we have now secured but they were certainly practices of the Hebrews, who are supposed to have had a special revelation or a genius for morality, throughout almost the whole of their history.

CHAPTER III

THE GOLDEN AGE OF TEMPLE PROSTITUTES

IT is usual in such sketches as we have of the history of prostitution or of morals to pass at once from Egypt and Babylonia to Greece and Rome. The writer thus experiences a crescendo of virtuous horror and points out that, since the old world had sunk into a planet-wide debauch, a new moral gospel to the race was imperatively needed. We have, we saw, few references to prostitution in the older empires; and many do not reflect that this is largely due to the fact that they have left us no historical and social literature like that of the Greeks and Romans. But we have a very extensive literature about prostitution in Greece and Rome, and, while I am not prepared to say that the system flourished more luxuriantly than during the later Middle Ages, it certainly assumed proportions which are not surpassed by any other civilization. So we find even historians reproducing the familiar rhetoric about this final proof that the old world had not in itself a sufficient moral or social inspiration.

I have elsewhere exposed the gross fallacies of this literary tradition. It ignores the fact that during the six centuries before Christ the ascetic reaction which is said to be characteristic of Christianity was steadily developing in every part of civilization, appearing in the Buddhists and Jainists of India and the Zoroastrians of Persia and all the Persian, Greek, Hebrew, and Egyptian ethical codes which they inspired. It willfully confuses the genuine social interests of the race with sectarian ideas of sin and mistakes symptoms of a robust independence for signs of degeneration and national decay. Above all, and this chiefly concerns me here, it fails to take into account—indeed it is wholly ignorant of—a world-movement of the first millennium before Christ which is still ignored or misrepresented in general history. This movement we glimpsed when I described the Persians, after their conquest of Asia Minor, rapidly developing a luxury and amorous freedom which made a mockery of their sacred book and passing on their new ways to the

Babylonians. But again I will save space by assuming that the great majority of my readers have learned the facts from my earlier writings: in this case, particularly, the third volume of my **Story of Human Morals, The Phallic Ancient Civilizations.** There I fully describe a phase of history which is usually condensed into a paragraph or dismissed with a few ethical expletives yet is essential to the understanding of the story of prostitution and sex-morals generally in Greece, Alexandria, and Rome.

One usually reads, if one finds any notice of it, that contact with the "effete" peoples of Syria and Asia Minor infected the new civilizations of Persia, Greece, and Rome. The historical fact is that these smaller peoples of Syria and Asia Minor became powerful enough to wreck, or help to wreck, the older empires, and in their few centuries of prestige they communicated to a very large part of their world their cult of a goddess of love and fertility, with consecrated prostitutes, and the general candid attitude toward sex which such religion had given them. From Syria and eastern Asia Minor this cult spread to Phoenicia and Palestine, if not to Babylon and Egypt, to the Greeks of Asia Minor and Corinth, to south Italy, and along the north coast of Africa to Spain. Nation after nation eagerly embraced the gospel of love, and sacred prostitution flourished from Carthage to Mesopotamia, or over the entire civilized world. When the Greeks, and later the Romans, spread over this world they inevitably adopted an attitude toward sex which differed materially from that of their more sober ancestors or of the priests and prophets of the older civilizations. The sun or sky deity of the Persians had led aged and brooding recluses of that race to imagine a melodramatic contrast of light and darkness, virtue and vice, spirit and flesh. But the old mother-earth goddess made, if I may speak poetically, a last effort to regain the hearts of men, and she won an amazing success.

The facts about this remarkable spread of consecrated prostitution, which does much to explain the attitude of the Greeks and Romans, may here be briefly summarized. There is good reason to believe that the cult of the mother-goddess, with prostitute-priestesses, was quite general in the civilized area before and at the dawn of history. That area spread, it will be remembered, from Crete, through Asia Minor (with an extension to Egypt) and Mesopotamia, to India. The four greater civilizations, the Cretan, Egyptian, Sumerian, and Hindu, apparently outgrew, or at the most retained only feeble traces of, the idea that goddesses were particularly conciliated by such practices. Originally, perhaps, the practice was based on the magical idea of promoting fertility, and it is in just the area I have described that agriculture was developed and pastoral life first conducted on a large scale. The subject is too complex to be discussed here, but one can broadly understand how the more advanced civilizations and their male priesthoods would come to resent temple-prostitution. The less advanced civilizations of the Hittites (in Asia Minor) and of Syria and Palestine, with powerful bodies of priestesses as well as priests, retained *it,* and they rose to world-prominence as the older empires decayed and men began to travel extensively.

The chief centers were in the Hittite cities of eastern Asia Minor, some of which were "holy cities" in the sense that they were wholly dedicated to the goddess Ma and her priestesses. I have shown elsewhere how these priestesses, who wore a military equipment on festive occasions, gave the Greeks their story of Amazons, and I have gathered together such scanty accounts of them as we have. It is enough to recall here that the Greek geographer Strabo found, as late as the first century B. C., that the temples and priestesses of Ma were still famous. In two cities he found that there were no less than six thousand ministers of ₊the chief temple (in each), and that of these "many were women, mostly sacred, who live by their bodies." At the festivals of the goddess streams of visitors came from Armenia and other outlying lands. The temples were extremely wealthy, and the citizens generally had a h'gh standard of luxury. Vineyards covered a very large part of the country, and refined banquets were highly appreciated.

It is only in recent history that we appreciate the power and significance of the Hittite civilization, and we are not now surprised that its cult of a mother-goddess was shared and adopted over the entire region. In Armenia, Strabo says, the goddess Anaitis had equal importance. Ladies of free birth, often of the best families, voluntarily prostituted themselves to strangers at her temples, and their prestige rose with their success in adding to the funds of the temple by their amorous services. The more assiduous they were during the temporary period of ministry, the more eagerly they were sought in marriage. To the south, in Cappadocia, was another famous temple with three thousand male and female ministers, and it seems that part of these also earned money for the temple by consecrated prostitution.

Some recent writers strain the evidence to show that this cult of a fertility-goddess was native to the Semitic peoples. I prefer to think that, as I said in the case of the Hebrews, their milder interest in agriculture, since they were mostly desert-nomads, had not directed their religion along those lines. It is not until the time of the Christian Fathers that we learn of temple-prostitution in Arabia itself, though the general attitude to sex was naturalistic enough. But wherever the Semites settled in agricultural regions, they, like the Hebrews, readily adopted the cult of love. It is quite time that historians ceased to speak of the Syrians as "degenerate" and "effete" because of their great love-temples, while they describe the Semitic Hebrews, with just the same religion, as robust and progressive.

But I have in earlier works described both the people and the ceremonies at their temples, in Syria and northern Phoenicia. At Hierapolis-Bambyce, on the upper Euphrates, or within the range of Persia and Babylonia, the mother-goddess, here known as Attar, was honored by the prostitution of women in her temple. At Hierapolis (later Baalbek) in Palestine the Phoenician name Ashtart (Ishtar) was given to the goddess; and in the early centuries of the

Christian Era the Fathers complain sombrely of wild sexual orgies, to the music of drums and sistra, on the nights of her festivals. They say that every maid was required to prostitute herself in honor of Ashtart, but many believe that more probably there were permanent priestesses, as in Asia Minor, or temporary and voluntary ministers, as in Armenia. In northern Phoenicia, at Byblos, there was an even more famous center of consecrated prostitution, at the temple of Tammuz (Adonis). When, in the holy week, the priests announced the resurrection of Tammuz, all women who had not sacrificed their hair to the god, which seems to have been the alternative for conscientious objectors, came forward to prostitute themselves to the vast crowds of visitors. There seem to have been few who objected, for women were honored in proportion to their diligence in earning money for the temple.

The world had become more cosmopolitan during this first millennium before Christ, and there was more traveling than there had ever been before. Streams of men of a dozen nationalities converged upon these famous shrines for their greater festivals or upon the permanent centers of prostitution, where the temples were museums of art and the cities were very attractive. Travelers by land and sea took the news of their experiences, and settlements of Syrians and others in foreign cities reproduced the institutions of their religion. It is probable that in the great city of Sidon, or on the hills above it, temples of Ashtart were surrounded by huts or tents in which, or in its encircling groves, consecrated women plied their trade. And the same Phoenicians, the most daring navigators and most enterprising merchants of the time, carried the cult far across the Mediterranean. The city of Carthage which they founded devoted itself more particularly to their grim masculine deity, but near it was the settlement of Sicca Veneria where the temple of the goddess looked down upon the little homes of the industrious ministers of love. Even in the time of St. Augustine the Christian opposition had not yet entirely conquered the goddess of love. At the festivals of Tanit at Carthage, which he witnessed, the "sacred virgins" of its goddess, he says, were quite "obscene" in their songs and dances. From the southern shore of the Mediterranean the enterprising Phoenician merchants had crossed to Italy, the south of France, and Spain, and we find traces of the cult here and there. Strabo says that there was in his time a great temple of the oriental Venus at Eryx, in Sicily, which had formerly had large numbers of consecrated prostitutes.

Along two other lines of advance the cult of love spread to meet and influence the Greeks. One was over the islands of the Mediterranean. I have fully described elsewhere the rites of the great temple at Paphos, in Cyprus, where every woman had to minister in the service of the goddess before marriage. It is often suggested that this practice was the original form of temple-prostitution, and that the restriction of the service to a body of priestesses was an advance upon it. In my opinion the reverse of this is true. The greed of the priests—in most cases masculine priests were at the head of all—discovered that their revenues from this source increased if the fresh maids of the entire community were available instead of a body of priestesses who grew old in the service. However that may be, the temple at Paphos, a superb and prominent building on the main lines of Mediterranean shipping, was famed in every port. At the other end of Cyprus there was a temple of Ashtart with male, and probably also female, prostitutes. The whole beautiful island seemed to the Greeks to be devoted to the glorification of love, and there was not a sailor, traveler, or merchant who did not visit it and help to spread the fame of its temples.

The progress of the cult across Asia Minor was the most important of all. That region of which people now think only as the obscure and half-barren home of the Turks, has played a very important part in the development of ethical ideas. It was, as I said, the chief area of the cult of the great Ma (Mother), and it profoundly modified the sex-ethic of the Persians and Greeks. It was from Asia Minor, too, that the ascetic reaction against phallic religion spread; just as the fiercest Socialist protests are heard where wealth displays its most criminal extravagance. From it came to Europe, first the Pythagorean puritans, next the Mithraists and Manichaeans, and then Paul of Tarsus and his associates. It was chiefly Asia Minor that spread the gospel of love in the immediately pre-Christian world; and it was mainly from the same regions that the champions of the sky-god set out to challenge it and confuse the mind and practice of the race during the next two thousand years.

The phallic temples of the Hittites which I have described were in the far east of the region, but there is good evidence that the religion had at one time covered the whole of Asia Minor. In fact, the Cretans of the west were at one with the Hittites in cherishing a supreme mother-goddess, and we must suppose that during the third and second millennia before Christ prostitution, either consecrated or genially respected, flourished over the whole region from southern Italy to Mesopotomia. In the second millennium a wedge of Aryans drove down into Asia Minor from the north, and the nations of the Lydians and Phrygians were formed. These frankly adopted the religion of love, or the glorification of sense and sex to which it led, and it was contact with them that civilized the Greeks and helped to develop their remarkably candid attitude toward sex.

Sir William Ramsay, the chief authority on the history of ancient Asia Minor, tells us that at Tralles in Lydia sacred prostitution was still an "honorable practice for women of good birth" in the second century of the Christian Era. But the Lydians had skeptically removed the stricter religious element from the gospel of love and developed its human element. I fully described their remarkable civilization in the third volume of the **Story of Human Morals,** and it deserves to be better known. The Lydians were the most joyous of all peoples in that ancient world. Their cooks, musicians, dancers, and courtesans were equally famous in the Greek world until, in the sixth century, the puritan Cyrus wantonly destroyed their civilization. They had temple-prostitutes, though no self-castrating priests or other somber features of the cult, and every girl who was not rich earned her dowry either in the temple or elsewhere. Prostitution was an honorable occupation, and the pleasure-quarters of their cities were, not squalid districts to be shunned by decent men, but open and merry settlements in the woods, known to all as "The Good Corner."

Their Aryan neighbors the Phrygians took the cult of the mother-goddess more seriously—see my **Story of Human Morals** for full details—yet, by a strange accident of history, it was their form of the cult of the Great Mother (Cybele) that was adopted by the frivolous Romans. They had temple-prostitutes everywhere, and their influence on the historical development of religion is curiously illustrated by the fact that the "Holy Week" of the Roman Church is in a large sense based upon theirs. But here it is more important to appreciate the influence of the gayer and much more powerful Lydians. The contemptuous neglect of them by historians of ancient times—very few people know even that Croesus, whose name we still use as a symbol of wealth, was king of Lydia—is partly responsible for the misunderstanding of the development of the Greeks. To the early Greeks the Lydian capital, Sardis, was one of the greatest and most attractive cities of the world, and it was Croesus who mastered and raised to a high degree of civilization the famous cities of Asia Minor (Miletus, Ephesus, etc.) in which the Greeks first learned to cultivate art, science, and letters. The western coast of Asia Minor, where Greek civilization began, was drenched with Lydian influence. Hence the wonderful development of lyrical and amorous poetry (Sappho, etc.) in the north, and the appearance of sages and moralists in the rich commercial cities of the south.

The Greeks reacted in various ways to this gospel of the free and sensuous life with which they came into contact in Asia Minor while Athens was still a town of no importance. We see two extremes in the great temple of Aphrodite at Corinth, where a thousand temple-prostitutes gave the tone to the entire city, and the great temple of Diana at Ephesus, where the older Greek superstition prevailed over the phallic idea and the priestesses were chaste. We see an intermediate position in the Greek philosophers and moralists, who generally taught sobriety or temperance but in nearly every case approved prostitution and had liberal sentiments in regard to sex. The mass of the race, and especially their artists and poets, who gave the first high distinction to the Greeks, frankly adopted the gospel of love.

I will try to trace their development in the next chapter, but the reader will now see what important elements of explanation are lost when historians neglect those peoples of Asia Minor and Syria. The process of the civilization of the Greeks may be put between 1000 and 500 B. C. That was the golden age of temple-prostitution, of extreme naturalism in sentiments about sex; and it was with one of the most sensuous and amorous of all the peoples of the time that the raw Greeks first came into contact. I have made this chapter short because I have given the details elsewhere, and a

summary view is the most useful here. Driven out of their barren
and over-populated and narrow-minded home, the Greeks streamed
over the sea in vast numbers, and they found everywhere great
temples of love and free-living peoples. At Eryx in Sicily and near
Carthage, on the islands of the Mediterranean, in the cities of the
coast and the immediate interior of Asia Minor, on the south coast
of Asia Minor and the coasts of Syria and Phoenicia, the outstanding
shrine and place of pilgrimage, enriched by centuries of art and
luxury, was a temple of the divinity who had inspired and now
smiled upon the amorous relations of men and women. This, apparently, was civilization. Not until a later date would philosopher-
travelers go beyond and learn what men thought in the far-distant
cities of Persia, Babylonia and Egypt. When we study this education of the Greek, we dispense with the superficial theory that he
was innately more sensuous or immoral than others. But I am not
here concerned with theories. I am substituting sound history for
the ragged account of facts which at the most speaks of a temple
of love at Paphos or Byblos and does not give the reader the faintest
appreciation of the remarkable spread of prostitution, largely in the
name of religion, in the millennium before Christ.

Let me add two final reflections. The first is that the reader
ought now to perceive how shallow and false is the customary cry,
that these robust and sober Greeks and Romans were infected by
contact with "the effete and degenerate east." The Lydians and
Phoenicians, with whom they chiefly came into educational contact,
were as robust as themselves. They were at that time the missionaries of civilization, the finest craftsmen and most enterprising merchants. The oldest city of that world, where the moral rhetorician
might plausibly speak of degeneration, was "rose-colored Damas-
cus," and it was probably the last to be visited by Greeks and was,
in any case, not famous for temple-prostitution. But these vagaries
of moralist historians are very largely based upon ignorance of
the facts of sexology. One generally finds that when they speak
of the "nameless vices of the worn-out east" which the Greeks and
Romans are supposed to have acquired in age-old cities of the east—
some writers mention Antioch and Alexandria, which were then no
more ancient than New York now is—they mean such a practice
as sodomy : which is, and always was, more common amongst robust
savages and barbarians than in cities. But the question does not
arise. Roman soldiers learned far more in Antioch and Alexandria
and Corinth, which were only a few centuries old, than in such
really ancient cities as Thebes and Babylon.

The second point is that the candor in sexual matters which
the Greeks learned from the Lydians was not accompanied by any
element that would lead to social deterioration. The Lydians were
not only one of the most vigorous and prosperous peoples of the
time, but it was really they, not the Hebrews, who raised the Golden
Rule, as the Chinese did, to the rank of first place in the moral
code. Friendliness to all—the only sensible form of the Golden
Rule—was their first principle: the first (and often only) virtue
that they carved on a man's tombstone. I have elsewhere shown

that it was most probably from them that the idea of trade unions of the workers came to the Greeks and Romans and that Epicurus derived his ideal of friendship. To them, indirectly, we can trace the Stoic ideal of brotherhood which, blended with the Epicurean, transformed the Roman world. But I have proved all these things elsewhere, and we must get back to our brothels. The first moral requirement of our age is to insist on truthfulness in our moral-historical literature.

CHAPTER IV

THE GREEKS HUMANIZE PROSTITUTION

I KNOW nothing more ludicrous in serious modern literature than the attempt of so many writers to sustain the note of superiority when they speak of the ancient Greeks. Such defects as there were in the Greek civilization I have freely acknowledged, but the Greeks played, in proportion to the duration of their power and the extent of their race, a part in the advance of the race that no other nation, ancient or modern, ever played. In our freer age this is frequently claimed by our most learned Hellenists, but works constantly appear in which the author ignores, or is ignorant of, their remarkable contribution to social, intellectual, and aesthetic progress and, on the ground of some supposed ethical defect, represents them as inferior, not only to ourselves, but to the nations of medieval Europe. And this ridiculous charge is chiefly based upon the extent and organization of prostitution in the Greek world. A few moralists might protest that they refer more particularly to sodomy, but the most distinguished Hellenists discredit the evidence on which they rely, and I have shown that the practice is far more common in modern Greece, and southern Europe generally, than we know it to have been in ancient Greece.

It is particularly urged against the Greeks that even their moralists failed to denounce prostitution. Let us first understand this. It is quite true that scarcely any of the Greek moralists condemned intercourse with unmarried women, and therefore, since, like the leaders of every other civilization, they wished their young women to live chastely until they married, they were compelled at least to look leniently upon the existence of a body of professional women. That is merely to say that they adopted the social ethic to which our age is fast returning. When Socrates heard that the courtesan Theodota was remarkable for her beauty, he went to visit her and in the most friendly manner discussed her mode of life. Xenophon tells us in his Memorable Things that Socrates advised youth to avoid the more beautiful prostitutes, if they would avoid ruin, and be content with the plainer and cheaper; and in his Banquet (IV., 38) he puts into the mouth of the sage these words:

If at times my body requires venereal satisfaction, any woman who is available satisfies me.

Plato, although his mind was more complicated by Persian and Egyptian mysticism, was never decisive against fornication. He thought (**Phaedo**) that followers of philosophy ought to be superior to these sensual pleasures : that it was, for civic reasons, better that men and women should "pair like the birds, not promiscuously" (**Laws**) : that men should be faithful to their wives until the child-bearing age is over, and then he would permit straying (**Republic**). In other words he alleged civic reasons, but he slightly complicated them by his ascetic theory of spirit and flesh. Aristotle (in his **Politics**) advised strict monogamy in the family-rearing age but granted freedom before and after it. The early and genuine Stoics did not condemn fornication. Indeed, the chief Greek writer on the philosophers, Diogenes Laertius, gives a story that Zeno occasionally, and on cold principle, had relations with his servant, to prove that his sect was not in this respect puritanical. In short, Pythagoras alone—to ignore the dreamy thinkers who were later called Neo-Platonists—condemned all such intercourse, and for the good reason that he had adopted the ascetic Persian idea that all flesh was evil. It is said that ten of his militant disciples once, after a defeat, might have saved their lives by crossing a beanfield, but they died rather than tread on beans, which to the Greeks had a phallic significance.

Many of the Greek moralists had, contrary to a common opinion, a deep and extensive influence, sometimes virtually ruling entire cities. We must not judge them by the small influence of Plato and Aristotle in Athens. But they were to the extent of nine-tenths materialists, and their ethic was generally social. Later Greek writers assigned mistresses to nearly all of them, but, except that Aristotle took to his home the beautiful courtesan Herpyllis after the death of his wife, we cannot regard these as reliable statements. It is enough that they did not condemn intercourse with the unmarried, and they therefore saw that there must be either a general freedom of girls before marriage, which was deeply repugnant to Greek traditions, or a large body of professional women. Thus they approved of the supervision and taxation of prostitutes by the state. Whether the world became "cleaner" or in any sense better when they were displaced as guides of the race by the followers of Paul we shall see later.

This question of the moralists is so commonly thrust into the foreground in any discussion of Greek prostitution that I dispose of it first. But the more important consideration is that with which I closed the last chapter : the fact that nearly every civilization with which the Greeks came into contact in the course of their education glorified sexual love. We may confidently assume that for many centuries after their settlement on the Mediterranean the Greeks had no prostitution, or that there was merely an isolated figure here and there who might be called a prostitute. In so far as the Homeric poems reflect the semi-barbaric days, we find the leaders so free in the use of concubines and female slaves that nothing further was needed. It was the growth of towns which led to the institution. Whether, as Greek legend says, the stern legislator Draco had to curb the growth of prostitutes in Athens as early as the seventh century, the wiser Solon gathered the women in a state-brothel at the Piraeus (five miles away) and imposed a tax and civic infamy on them, and the aristocratic sons of Peisistratus reopened Athens to them and encouraged them, scholars are not now agreed. What we do know is that the temple of Aphrodite at Corinth, with its thousand consecrated prostitutes, existed before the year 500 B. C., for the girls were specially deputed to implore the favor of the goddess at the time of the Persian invasion, and the grateful city had a picture painted of the white-robed ladies offering incense to their patroness and begging her mediation with Zeus; much as French nuns implored Mary to intercede for France in 1914. Another illustration of the fact that their ministry was widely respected in Greece is that in 464 B. C. a competitor at the Olympian games named Xenophon vowed, if he won, to present "a certain number" (not a thousand, as one often reads) of maids to the temple; and they were afterwards consecrated in his presence, the great poet Pindar composing an ode for the solemn occasion.

There is other evidence that by the sixth century prostitution was well developed, not only in the colonial cities of Asia Minor, Egypt (as we saw), and south Italy, but in most of the Greek cities of the mainland. In Sparta it was never an institution. The married women themselves were so free in their conduct that brothels were unnecessary. But in Athens and most other cities the painted vases of the time, which tell us so much of the early life, show that the professional women were already a prominent feature. Nude men and women are seen in attitudes or dances that plainly belong to the life of the brothel. On one a nude woman holds in her hands a phallus: on another a man hands a purse to a flute-player. The development was plainly checked by legislation, whether or no the author was Solon. It was enacted that the women must live in brothels under state-supervision and pay a small tax. It is said that Solon built a temple from the proceeds of the tax; just as in the Middle Ages it was at times used for the building of churches. The women were registered and were outlaws in the sense that they had no rights of citizenship, could not marry citizens, and their children carried the same disabilities. This legal "infamy" lasted during the whole of Greek history until the Christian Emperor Justinian modified it (so that he could marry a prostitute), and it must be borne in mind by those who dwell upon the supposed complete moral indifference of the Greeks to prostitution. The women could not even secure common justice in the courts, and they were often wrongly charged with impiety or dishonesty, until, in the fourth century, the beautiful Phryne won a case by her champion, the orator Hyperides, stripping off her upper garments and exhibiting her shoulders and bust to the judges. The ordinary Greek did not, in most ages, step into a brothel as jauntily as into his tailor's; and there is a story of a young girl bursting into tears when she learns that her elder sister has adopted one of the more respectable branches of the profession.

But these registered and generally despised prostitutes of the brothels were only one section of the entire body. Informed writers usually distinguish four classes, besides the consecrated prostitutes of Corinth: the famous hetairai, the flute-players, the inmates of the brothels, and the crowds of unlicensed prostitutes who evaded the police and generally plied their humble trade, for a fee of a few cents, in the dark streets and squares. To take the higher class first, the hetairai, I need add little here to what I have already written about them. The English word "pal" or "chum" is the nearest equivalent to the word hetairai, and it is occasionally used by Greek girls in that innocent sense, while in late Greek writers it is often applied to courtesans generally. The truth is that there was no class sharply distinguished from respectable Greek women on the one hand or from the professional prostitutes on the other. Rhodopis of Naucratis was, as I said, a slave inmate of a brothel who, after being purchased by Sappho's brother, became one of the most famous and wealthy of the hetairai. Particularly pretty or accomplished flute-players, like Lamia, often rose to the higher category. They were prostitutes in the full sense of the word, though they at times became the exclusive mistresses of rich men or princes. On the other hand, many very accomplished women were included in the class of hetairai, although, even if they had free ideas about sex, they were certainly not prostitutes. Whether the famous Aspasia was at first a prostitute (as her enemies said) we do not know, but she certainly was not in the period when the scholars, artists, and statesmen of Athens gathered round her at the house of Pericles. Numbers of the women who passed as hetairai were teachers of philosophy or rhetoric, or authors, and there is no proof whatever that they took money for love.

The reason for this vagueness is well known. The Greek was bored by the ignorance and lack of interests which custom imposed upon his wife, and he was unable to invite male friends, as even a Roman might, to enjoy a meal with his wife and daughter. Just at the time when education created this gulf between the Athenian and his wife, the freer and more accomplished Greek women from colonial cities began to settle and earn their living in wealthy Athens. They were prevented by law from marrying Athenians, and they remained the unmarried "pals" of the educated men or entered into non-legal unions like that of Pericles and Aspasia. One has a fair parallel in the educated but unmarried and independent ladies who, in New York or Chicago, freely receive us in their apartments and dine with us. As a body the hetairai, in the strict sense of the word, are most improperly called courtesans or prostitutes, though they often had lovers. The article on them in the Encyclopaedia of Religion and Ethics, which speaks contemptuously of their "world of superficial accomplishments, tawdriness, vulgarity, and heartlessness" lamentably fails to distinguish the real hetairai from the broad class which later bore the name. Even the learned and lengthy article on them by Professor K. Schneider in Pauly's Lexikon fails to make this clear. All these writers follow the work of Athenaeus, the Deipnosophists (Book XIII), which was written centuries later and uses the word hetaire as synonymous with mistress or courtesan.

The famous beauties whose lives are quoted from his pages—
Phryne, Thais, Lamia, Bacchis, Lais, Glycera, Pythonice, etc.—
were adventuresses of a later date.

We cannot draw a strict line because the early body of independent women who came from Ionia or other regions to seek a
livelihood in Athens was, when the city became rich and famous,
merged in a larger class of adventurers, large numbers of whom
were partially or entirely higher courtesans. The great general
Themistocles, son of a courtesan, is said to have driven through
Athens in the first quarter of the fifth century with four famous
courtesans in his chariot; though some scholars think that this
daring flouter of conventions was really Alcibiades. Certainly by
the time of Pericles there was in Athens a large body of the wealthier independent courtesans who began to be called **hetairai.** It was
at this period that the Greeks generally adopted a more liberal attitude toward prostitution. Most of these women lived in the elegant
Ceramic quarter, near the city wall, and they were well known to
all generally by nicknames which were not always flattering and
were often ingenuous (Callipyge, for instance, which I must translate by a paraphrase, "Very pretty on the rear view"). Several
hundred of these names have survived. When a man desired to
open up negotiations with one, he wrote her name on the wall,
probably with a flattering epithet. The ladies, as is the custom of
their class, lay abed to noon, and their slaves had then a busy hour
or two over the bath and toilet. One of the slaves went out to
scan the names on the wall, and it became the custom for courtesans
—except the more famous—to stand near the name until the man
appeared. The popularity of the quarter attracted large numbers
of women of the independent class, and the groves and colonnades
in which it abounded were used by them at night. There was, of
course, no illumination.

This class of independent prostitutes was so large and varied
that fees ranged from about five drachmas (roughly, a dollar) to
thousands of drachmas. Lais asked the famous orator Demosthenes,
who zealously cultivated the class, a prohibitive fee of ten thousand
drachmas (about $2,000); and the same lady, in her drunken later
years, was seen wandering about the quays of Corinth trying to
find a sailor who would pay her three oboli (say, a dime). One
lady has survived in history under the name Didrachmon, which
may be translated Miss Half-Dollar. The younger and more handsome generally exacted one or two gold pieces (five to ten dollars).
The choice few often asked ten times that sum; and the more famous
beauties, who often became the temporary mistresses of very rich
men, made very large fortunes. Demetrius, a Syrian Greek who
became virtual king of Athens after the death of Alexander, and
who brought the celebrated flutist Lamia to Athens, one day gave
her, "to buy soap," he said, a sum equivalent to a quarter of a million
dollars that he had levied on the city. We must remember that,
although we can express the Greek coins in modern terms, money
then purchased far more than it now does, and that men had to give
their favorites constant presents in addition to the fee.

The more detailed evidence about them is found in the thirteenth book of Athenaeus, and many authors who borrow from it seem to forget that he was an Egyptian Greek of the second century after Christ. Much of what he says may be gossip about earlier ages: much refers to Alexandria under the gay Ptolemies or Athens after the fall of the Republic. It was generally in this later period that some of the more famous courtesans had statues erected to them in the public squares or coins struck in their honor, or even received divine honors after death. The princes who succeeded Alexander and inherited the vast wealth of his empire were, after the example of Alexander, their most generous patrons. Phryne had a golden statue in the temple of Delphi. The tomb of Pythonice at Babylon cost $50,000 to build; and it was not the most princely monument of a courtesan. The inhabitants of Lampsacus bestowed a gold laurel wreath on Pharsalia, and more than one city built a temple of Aphrodite in honor of a famous courtesan. In the days of their prosperity the ladies spent vast sums on the decoration of their cities, and, since philosophers, artists, and statesmen treated them with respect, one cannot wonder at their prestige. Socrates himself, we saw, paid a friendly visit to Theodota. Demosthenes spent his large income on them. Praxiteles and other sculptors immortalized them in marble. Apelles, the greatest painter of antiquity, bought and trained the celebrated Lais, whom he found in her early years a Sicilian captive and slave. Gnathena gave banquets to which all Athenian society sought admission, and her witty sayings were treasured for centuries. Phryne, who won their charter of rights by her beauty, took the leading part in the religious pageant of Athens at the festival of Neptune, the entire city breaking into wild applause when, quite nude, she entered the water and offered sacrifice to the god.

These were the choicest beauties in several centuries of a score of nations, and the Greek athletic system for girls and love of open-air dancing, as well as the high aesthetic standards which the artists diffused, made beautiful girls numerous in the Greek world. Athenaeus tells us of all the tricks with which the ladies with less perfect figures covered their defects: how they raised their height by padding their sandals or lowered it by exercise in lowering the head; how the thin padded their haunches and the stout wore corsets; how those who did not easily laugh and show their teeth kept sprigs of myrtle in their mouths, and so on. Of their dress and cosmetics it would take long to tell. As these independent courtesans evaded the police, who at registration time tried all the devices of the modern police to bring them into the tax-paying system, they did not observe the regulation that they must wear a particular type of florid dress, to distinguish them from the maids and matrons. But one easily recognized them, as they stood in large numbers by the gate or sat in the colonnades, by their bright colors and heavy use of cosmetics. Solicitation in public was not allowed, and many of them had verses of love-songs stamped or cut on the soles of their sandals. One girl left on the pavement the words "Follow me" at every step she took.

Another very large class, apart from the registered inmates of
brothels, were the flute-players and dancers, who were, after the
fashion learned from the Lydians, hired for private banquets. When
the guests were flushed with wine, the girls, generally in transparent silks, sometimes nude, entertained them. Their airs on the
flute are said to have thrown men into sensual frenzies, and their
dances were not those of ordinary Greek girls. The banquets often
lasted all night, and freedom was unrestrained. You might see one
lying on the table while rich young men enacted the legend of Zeus
and Danae. . . At dawn sometimes the whole intoxicated party
would pour noisily into the street. Most of the girls were slaves,
hired out for the purpose at a dollar a night, but the most sought
of them demanded a thousand dollars or more. Sometimes the host
bought the slave-flautists and put them up to auction at the close
of the banquet. But large numbers bought their freedom, or persuaded lovers to buy it, and rose to the rank of free courtesans. They
gave banquets of their own, to which men were not invited, and
they were not decorous. Quarrels about superiority in beauty of
breast, limb, etc., ended in candid exhibitions, sometimes fights.
The Athenians held that most of them were much more cordial with
each other than with men. Often they had houses of their own
and charged hundreds of dollars—fees are mentioned up to three
thousand dollars—for their services. A few, like Lamia, who was
the idol of Alexandria and its king before she was brought to Athens
by Demetrius, attained world-wide fame and immense fortunes.

The third class consisted of the registered inmates of the
brothels. The larger of these were not unlike the licensed houses of
many countries in our time, the girls, who were generally slaves,
reclining on couches in transparent robes or standing, nude, in
rows. There was music and dancing, and the girls had separate
rooms. The cheapest of the brothels, to which slaves, freedmen,
and soldiers went, charged only about ten to twenty cents. Sometimes a man paid a large sum for the exclusive use of one girl for
a year, when the sign "Occupied" remained permanently over her
door. The brothels were under municipal supervision, but they
had a sort of "right of refuge." A wife could not enter in search
of her husband or a creditor seek his debtor.

Most of the houses of women were opened by private enterprise, but the Greeks had little respect for the women (generally)
who kept these and none for the men who conducted the very extensive and well organized "white slave traffic." Girls were doubtless frequently kidnapped (as in Africa a few centuries ago) in
foreign lands, but we must not forget that there was slavery everywhere, and it was generally the daughters of slaves or exposed
babies who were bought and reared for the purpose. Elderly
courtesans, who had saved some of their money, often bought a
few such slave children and trained them to entertain. Some of
the larger brothels had schools attached, in which the girls learned
music, dancing, and other accomplishments. Men who entered the
trade were despised and mercilessly treated in the comedies, and
women often contented themselves with one or two girls whom.

they declared to be their daughters. The prostitute-tax was farmed out by the State, and the agents of the contractor were ever on the watch to bring independent harlots under registration. A particularly attractive girl might be-hired out for a time to or even bought (for from a thousand to three thousand dollars) by a fervent lover. All strove desperately to charm some rich visitor who would buy their freedom and enable them to enter the rank of the prosperous free courtesans. Some who were bought from a shipper or trader for from fifteen hundred to three thousand dollars were eventually sold for twenty thousand.

The lowest type of brothel, which no decent Athenian would enter, sold drink, and the place was squalid. Here, and in the taverns, the poorest types of women, and the worn-out women, sold their services for a dime, or for a meal and a bottle of wine. Others frequented the dark streets at night and earned a meal under the shelter of a building. At the Piraeus (the port for Athens, some five miles away) large numbers of the women reached this pathetic end of their careers, hiring themselves to the sailors. The great square at Piraeus, which opened upon the quays, swarmed with women at night, waylaying sailors and travelers. Here solicitation was unheeded, and the women went off, according to their type, to the brothel, the temple of Venus, the shadow of the Great Wall, or the open shore. It was the same at most of the Greek ports, and the richer maritime cities, like Corinth, and watering places, like Epidauros, had every type of courtesan.

At Corinth there was, as I said, a temple of Aphrodite with a thousand slave girls who ministered to every visitor. Aphrodite had many names, and in her particular role of patroness of courtesans there were a score of temples built in her honor in various parts of Greece. In this character she was not "Venus Pandemos" (which means the Venus of the Whole People or the Common People), as is often said. Modern scholars tell us that that statement is an anti-democratic libel of the puritan Plato. But, although she had an annual festival which was boisterously celebrated by the courtesans, it seems that temple-prostitution existed only at the very old foundation in a cypress grove at Corinth, where the priests clung to their revenues. The light-hearted Corinthians did not mind. Almost every house in the-beautiful city is said to have been more or less a temple of love. Every boarding-house keeper was ready to prostitute his daughters, or alleged daughters, and slaves, and touts met visitors as they descended from the boats at the quays. Ill-favored or aged women prowled at night; and in the marble mansions every type of courtesan and flute-player, up to the beautiful Lais, contributed to the gaiety of the nightly banquets.

Such, as far as modern conditions permit me to describe it, was the love-life of the Greek city, which spread between 600 B. C. and 400 A. D. to every part of the Graeco-Roman world, or to the whole area of civilization. While we must remember that we have a very abundant Greek literature and a very scanty literature of earlier civilizations, we may safely conclude that there had never before been such a development of prostitution. But we must guard ourselves against exaggerated impressions. I refrain from the customary epithets of "shameless," "debauched," etc., and merely repeat the fact that the Greeks as a body did not recognize that moral law forbade intercourse with unmarried women. And what our modern puritans so often fail to notice is that this mood of theirs permitted so extraordinary a development of prostitution largely, if not mainly, because they were bent on keeping their wives and daughters chaste. Again I refrain from discussing ethical values, but I would remind our moralists, who shudder at the picture I have drawn, that the other side of the picture is that the wives and daughters of the Greeks seem to have been far more virtuous, thanks to the system of prostitution, than in most other civilizations.

Let me make the point a little clearer, for the custom of presenting the facts I have here given as a picture of Greek "morals" not only misleads people as to the general character of the Greeks, which was high, but is often used to justify the statement that the Greeks had no idea of sexual virtue until they became Christians. For the real and high virtues of the Greeks I must refer to my Story of Human Morals. My present point may be illustrated by the case of Menander, the leading representative of the later or New Comedy. The Rev. Professor Mahaffy expressly selects him as illustrating the moral improvement which, he says, came over Athens in the fourth century B. C. "The refinement of Greek manners," he says, "culminated in the gentle Menander." He adds that many of the comedian's sentiments are "almost Christian," and he particularly exhibits pictures of decent and happy marriages. But this is just the period when prostitution was most developed in Athens, and Menander was a very generous patron of the courtesans. Moreover, this same period, when courtesans were most openly patronized, is just the period of the greatest thinkers and moralists of Athens. From that time onward prostitution was very free in the whole Greek world, yet it is the time when the more ascetic moralists begin to appear. These moralists kept their little groups apart from the general license as earnestly as did the early Christian leaders; and with no more effect upon public opinion. Decent Greeks resented the coarse features of the lower types of brothels as decent folk resent the squalor of prostitution in its lowest forms in a modern city. But they adhered to a social ethic which, while it forbade adultery as an infringement of rights, seemed to them to have no application to the intercourse of the unmarried. We may not consider that they found an ideal solution of what is narrowly called the social problem, but to charge them with moral obtuseness is absurd.

CHAPTER V.

THE WHORES AND COURTESANS OF ROME

THE history of prostitution has hitherto been so loosely and imperfectly written that writers on the subject give us quite contradictory estimates of the difference between the Greek and Roman varieties of it. We are told repeatedly, as it is the fashion for these writers to copy from each other, that the

Romans "sank far lower" than the Greeks, since they had not the same sense of decency and dignity to restrain them: that while in the case of the Greeks we may recognize a perverse aesthetic element, the materialistic Romans adopted the institutions of their neighbors and exploited them with a merely animal satisfaction. This tradition seems to have started with the passage in Lecky's History of European Morals:

> The extreme coarseness of the Roman disposition prevented sensuality from assuming that aesthetic character which had made it in Greece the parent of art and had very profoundly modified its influence. . . . There have certainly been many periods in history when virtue was more rare than under the Caesars, but there has probably never been a period when vice was more extravagant or uncontrolled.

Mr. Lecky does not continue his survey of European morals beyond the age of Charlemagne or he would have hesitated to say that the Roman imperial period was the coarsest or most extravagant in history. But against these verdicts on Rome one could place a large number from modern writers who say, as Professor Westermarck does, that the Romans "regarded the courtesan class with much contempt" or that "prostitutes were in all ages despised at Rome." It was, in fact, the popular Roman lecturer, Dion Chrysostum, who first demanded the suppression of prostitution by law, as he called for the abandonment of slavery: it was the Roman Stoic Musonius Rufus who denounced all extra-matrimonial intercourse as unlawful; and the asceticism of Marcus Aurelius is known to all.

All these generalizations, however, are as inept and assailable as it would be to generalize on the English character and pick your facts from any period between the coming of the Normans and the twentieth century. Let us see the facts. In what writers persist in calling the virtuous period, the early period, of Roman history there was no prostitution. What the morals of the poorer Romans, as the city grew, were we can conjecture but the virtue of the patrician consisted in having the free use of any of the numerous female slaves of his house as well as his wife. He was, we are told, saved from the temptation to set up a class of hetairai, as in Greece, by the fact that, though he had despotic power over his wife, and kept her out of public life, she was treated more liberally than in Greece and was a real companion. Possibly his own lack of any serious cultural interests until the third century is a better explanation; and, when the Greeks began to influence him in that century, prostitution was already a familiar institution at Rome. One of the most familiar figures in the comedies of Terence and Plautus is the prostitute: one of the most despised figures the procurer.

At what date a supervised system began in Rome we do not know, but the historian Tacitus describes the system as ancient. Such women, he says, must have their names entered on the Aedile's list "according to a recognized custom of our ancestors, who considered it a sufficient punishment of an unchaste woman to have to profess her shame." The truth is that, while the Greeks were much nearer to the free-living Lydians of Asia Minor, the Romans had an almost equally stimulating example in Italy. Not very far north of Rome was the ancient and still rather obscure civilization of the Etruscans, who had as cheerful a philosophy of life as the Lydians and Syrians. From them the Romans learned civilization, and the borrowing seems to have included a goddess of love, Venus, who was, Macrobius says, unknown at first to the Romans. However that may be, prostitutes were numerous and organized in Rome by the third century B. C. They registered their names and full particulars; and no abandonment of the trade released them from the infamy which they thus contracted. They paid a tax and were forbidden to wear the distinctive garments of the matron. If they ventured abroad in daylight, they must wear "a toga [male tunic] of dull color" (probably brown), display no jewelry, and dye their hair yellow (later red or blue) or wear a yellow wig. A lamp in the shape of a phallus hung over the door of the brothel, and those who considered themselves "decent" Romans, though not puritans, drew the corners of their cloaks over their faces when they entered.

When, in the third century, the doors of Rome were thrown wide open to the influence of the Greeks and orientals; when skepticism about the old Roman religion spread and Greek philosophy was cultivated; and especially when the successful career of world-conquest made Rome the richest city of the world and attracted every variety of luxury to it, the system of prostitution greatly expanded and was relieved, in the general relaxation of morals, of much of its infamy. Already in the comedies of Plautus we find the distinction between "good prostitutes" or "good women"—let us say courtesans—and the common scortum or "whore." By the middle of the first century B. C. we find the famous orator and moralist Cicero saying in one of his public orations (Pro Caelio, 48):

> But if there is any man who thinks that even the love of courtesans is forbidden to our youth, he is assuredly very strict, but he differs from both the freedom of our age and the customs and concessions of our ancestors. For when was it not done? When was it not permitted? When was there a time when what is now lawful was unlawful?

It is true that on occasion Cicero could scornfully fling at an opponent the epithet "whoremonger," but his attitude remained that of the overwhelming majority of the educated Romans. There were, as I said, a few ethical protests, but even the ascetic Epictetus is reported to have said:

> Concerning sexual pleasure, it is right to be pure before marriage, as much as in you lies. . . . But do not in any case make yourself disagreeable to those who use such pleasures.

In short, we must say in regard to the attitude of the different classes of the community just what we said in regard to Athens.

The chief difference of the system that developed in Rome was that the higher courtesans never reached the height that they did in Greece: the entertainers (flautists and dancers) never became nearly so numerous and prosperous, and they were almost entirely foreigners; and the lower type of prostitution had an abnormal development. Against the names of some two hundred courtesans that we gather from Greek literature we can set only the few temporary mistresses whose charms are sung, or their perfidy deplored, by such poets as Horace and Catullus. These were the select members of a fairly large class, however. Under the emperors they were generally permitted to ignore the legal restrictions, and, in bright silk robes and laden with jewels, they joined the procession of the wealthy in the Via Sacra. Black slaves bore the gold and ivory litters of the more successful, and the young men of the smart set hastened to kiss their fingers in sight of all Rome. Amongst the crowd of slaves who followed them was the inevitable scribe or steward, with whom business might be discussed. Instead of being despised, these ladies were glorified in the eyes of all Rome by the verse of the leading poets.

According to Mr. Sanger and many others these Roman courtesans differed also from the Greek in their practices. We are told that in the Epigrams of Martial, in which they and their clients are described or satirized, "pictures of revolting pruriency succeed each other rapidly": that the poets use words for which "a man would be turned out of a modern brothel" and describe sexual acts to which there is nothing corresponding in our own time. Dr. Sanger does not seem to have known Greek or the medieval languages of Europe as well as he knew Latin. It was not exceptionally rich in sexual terms. Dupowey indeed says, I do not know on what authority, that a certain superstition restrained the Romans from using sexual language even in their orgies and brothels: that the tabu went so far that when, in the prolonged banquet, a guest required a slave to bring a certain vessel to him—they did not leave the room—he must not name it but make a certain sign.

But the amount of nonsense that is written about Martial and Juvenal is tiresome. Instead of finding salacious pictures "succeeding each other rapidly" in the pages of Martial, you will, if you take the trouble to read him, find that "revolting" epigrams are few and far between. That he describes anything unknown in modern or medieval times is quite an absurd statement. I must not enter into detail—Sorge is fairly candid in his German work—but I defy any person to find in Martial what he will not find, as daily practices even of non-professional modern women in Paris, in Victor Marguerite's novel **La Garconne**. For a few additional dollars prostitutes in any modern city do everything that is described in Martial or is painted on the walls of brothels in Pompeii. Mr. Lecky says that "the unblushing, undisguised obscenity of the epigrams of Martial, the Romances of Apuleius and Petronius, and of some of the Dialogues of Lucian, reflected but too faithfully the spirit of the time." The time, he seems to have forgotten, was that of the Stoic emperors, which all historians admit to have been the most admirable in Roman history.

It does not seem to occur to some—indeed very many—writers

to reflect on the difference it might make in our own literature if we had, instead of presses which put out thousands of copies of books under the eyes of the police and churches, just a few writers circulating hand-written copies amongst their friends. I had occasion lately to write a biographical sketch of a friend of George Meredith. In his diary I found notes of his conversations with Meredith, and in one of these the famous novelist assured my friend that the publishers of the pious poet Wordsworth found amongst his papers at his death "a lot of unprintable erotic poetry." So, said the caustic Meredith, "the poet of the cathedral-aisle, once outside, kicks like a goat." To compare an uncensored literature with one that is published under the truncheons of the police is childish; and I repeat that nothing that Martial describes as a practice in a certain set of ancient Romans is not found also, as a modern practice in a certain set, in the pages of Mr. Havelock Ellis. As far as I can understand, these writers who find "unparalleled things" in Martial are chiefly thinking of Roman prostitutes who used the orgies. It is ludicrous. The practice is quite common amongst prostitutes everywhere.

Many readers doubtless care to have this explanation, as far as one is free to give it, of the fairly common statement that there are in certain Roman writers of whom you cannot now get a literal translation descriptions of sexual practices or orgies which are today unknown. On the contrary, there is less variety in Martial than in the description of modern morbid practices in the works of Krafft-Ebing, Bloch, and Havelock Ellis. In all ages prostitutes think out or copy from each other every possible variation of sexual stimulation and intercourse; and writers who are too "refined" to study these matters might stretch their refinement a little farther and be more scrupulous about the truth of their statements. All that was different in ancient Rome was the openness of the system of prostitution, especially male prostitution. You would meet in the open Forum or street some effeminate male, heavily oiled and painted, with long hair and earrings, and he would raise his middle finger with the other fingers closed, and perhaps scratch his head with it. Most Romans despised him. We do things differently. In a main street of West London at night a young man in smart evening dress accosts me—I speak of actual experience—with a lift of his eyebrows (but looking carefully around for the police); soldiers in the central park are notoriously available; and numbers of men and youths lurk in the dark open spaces or "heaths" of the suburbs of the English metropolis. I assume the same in America.

Let me further point out what allowance must be made for custom in these matters. In Christian Ireland, for instance, which most people imagine to have been very virtuous, it was not uncommon to see—there are still specimens—a carving of a nude woman in the conjugal position with her pudenda most blatantly exposed (the Sheila-na-gig), on the keystone of the arched door through which men, women and children entered a church; but in ancient Rome, where the phallus was openly exposed, the female organ was never carved or painted, even in brothels. In Ireland it was a charm against the evil eye: in Rome, to depict it was to invite evil. In the case of Rome, again, disgust is expressed because at the Floralia, or festival of Flora (the spring festival), the prostitutes walked in procession, in thin if not transparent robes, a band of trumpeters at the head, to the Circus, where they exhibited nude dances to the people; and the day doubtless ended in more license than usual. But not only were troops of nude prostitutes seen in official processions in the Christian Middle Ages, but these same ancient Romans crucified or banished many thousands of men and women in a stern and successful attempt to suppress the wild Bacchanalian festival and certain much more innocent irregularities connected at one time with the cult of Isis. Again, the mixed nude bathing in the great Roman Baths, where prostitutes could display their forms and secure clients, is heavily censured. The censors do not add that the same practice, with the same results, was common in the baths of medieval Europe, or that mixed nude bathing was habitual in the most innocent villages on the coast of Japan until our own time.

However, while it is useful to consider these points, one must understand that there was a remarkable candor about sex in ancient Rome, or in the whole Greco-Roman civilization, and much of the system of prostitution was sordid; as it inevitably is in its cheapest forms. Writers are careful not to illustrate this by quoting the early life of "St." Helena, the mother of the Emperor Constantine. It is frivolous to say that the facts are disputed. St. Ambrose himself, the great court-bishop of the next generation, says quite cheerfully in a funeral oration of an emperor that Helena was a converted stabularia. Other Christian writers speak of her as a caupronaria (inn-servant), and perhaps she changed from one to the other. But the stabulum and the inn were the vilest types of Roman brothels. The former word might be translated "stable," for such precisely was its appearance. A number of girls and women plied their trade in one poor room, without divisions or curtains, without beds or couches. They lay in straw on the floor. Naturally, only the lower prostitutes descended to this. But the inns or wineshops of the poorer type were almost as bad. Even decent wineshops had a brothel in the rear, and the common drinking places were squalid.

The formal registered brothels, under the supervision of the municipal officer, were themselves of many types. The best and dearest, in one of the more respectable wards of the city, were ordinary Roman houses of the better type. There was a large elegant central court, with a fountain and statues, and the lightly clad ladies here met their clients. The bedrooms opened from the court—such houses had usually only one story—and were small windowless rooms, the bronze lamps and furniture bearing the emblems of the profession. A cheaper class were tenement blocks in the seething suburbs between the hills, where the night-life was deafening. The phallus was painted or carved over the door, or the lamps might have that shape, and nude or lightly clad women—some meretriciously covered the breasts or face with a veil of gold cloth—waited in the various rooms. Above each was a tablet indicating the name and price, the word "Occupied" showing when it was turned round.

Sometimes there was a reception room, its walls painted with such pictures as we find in Pompeii (or in Paris, for that matter) today. They were compelled by law to close from daybreak until three in the afternoon, when work generally ceased. One Latin writer says that there were forty-six of these brothels in Rome in the time of Augustus. He must mean in a particular district, however. A more reliable figure, if one can rely at all on these figures, is that the police counted 31,000 prostitutes of all types in the time of Trajan. That, since the population was about a million, is not much larger than the proportion in London, also according to the police, at the beginning of the last century.

The great majority of the brothels were, of course, in private hands, and they were of every conceivable type. In some the owner or procurer bought young female slaves and stocked his house: in others he rented rooms to prostitutes. The fee might be only two or three cents or might run to tens of dollars. If a procurer were so fortunate as to secure a virgin slave, or a young girl fresh from the "nurseries" where exposed female infants were reared, he put outside his house branches of laurel and a brighter lamp than usual. We know of a case in which the tablet on such an occasion announced that the fee for defloration was thirty dolars, a four-dollar fee sufficing afterwards. The man was, after his act, crowned with laurel by the slaves of the house and wore the wreath proudly in the street. Independent prostitutes of a higher type, who walked silk-clad in the fashionable streets, using their eyes and fingers or putting a ring in their mouths—they were, as in Greece, not permitted to solicit—or using old women as touts, had their own rooms in the lofty tenement blocks. The only trouble from the police was that they evaded taxation, and the agents were as busy as the police of Chicago in watching and catching them.

In this class again there were very many varieties, for each of which the Romans invented a name. A strange group plied their trade on the Esquiline Hill, where nervous folk would not venture at night. There the thieves gathered and the slaves were buried (as on the Vatican), and prostitutes or old women went to gather certain herbs by moonlight, to mix them with the blood of a black sheep (some said the liver of children) and make philtres or (alleged) aphrodisiacs, in which there was a great trade. Men spoke darkly of the orgies on the mystic Esquiline by night. Large numbers sought customers in the fornices (hence "forniculum") or vaulted cellars under the houses or stores. The arch of the door was a few feet above the level of the street, and, if you passed at night you might hear the rings of the curtain across the doorway rattle. The nude prostitute behind it thus advertised herself. Under the stands of the great Circus, a vast building which held 400,000 people, there were large numbers of these vaults or cells, and on festivals the women were very busy there. Others haunted the temples of Venus and Priapus, where solicitation was open, or lounged in the marble halls or corridors of the Baths, where the police saw to public decency. Some showed themselves on balconies of their houses, and very many used the cellars of bakers and other traders. Bakers, like barbers and perfumers, were very commonly bawds; which may not be unconnected with the fact that on the festivals of the phallic gods they made vast numbers of cakes in the shape of the phallus to sell to the crowds. Then there were the numerous streetwalkers of the more common type—"the Two-centers," the cheaper were called—who waylaid men in the unlit streets and retired to the shade of a building or a cemetery, or hung about the bridges and roads outside the walls.

I need not go into further detail, since all these things have analogies in a modern city, but in reflecting on this remarkable extent of prostitution in ancient Rome one must not forget the peculiar conditions. While the law and public sentiment drastically forbade adultery or seduction at most periods of Roman history, neither these nor religion nor the general moral sense condemned recourse to prostitutes as such. Sex was familiar to all from birth. At the Floralia even a child would see nude or half-nude prostitutes, and at the Lupercalia nude young men who, on an ancient custom, ran about the streets merrily striking matrons to promote fertility. The phallic emblem was carved or painted over brothels, and even in private houses the frescoes treated sex very naturalistically. Here piety forbade prudery, for the adventures of the gods and goddesses were largely amorous. But one must especially remember that Rome under the emperors had between quarter and half a million free workers who received free bread (or corn), medical service, schooling, entertainment, etc. They had, relatively, a large sum to spare for luxuries. Then there were the soldiers, the provincial visitors, the foreign sailors at the quays, and, above all, some hundreds of thousands of freedmen and domestic slaves (who could not legally marry). One can hardly wonder that there was such a development of the coarser forms of prostitution.

At the other end of the social scale, we are told, there was a laxity of sentiment as regards prostitution that one will not find in any other civilization. The proofs of this are, curiously enough, taken from the imperial edicts which set a limit to such laxity. The first emperor, Augustus, decreed that Roman citizens could not marry prostitutes; and it was a Christian emperor, Justinian, who removed the ban. The moral critics of Rome are so desperate that they first ask us to reflect on the appalling condition of a society in which it was necessary to forbid marriage with prostitutes and then ask us to admire the Christian charity to the fallen which removes the disability. But the next imperial edict is even worse abused. No writer touches the subject of the morals of ancient Rome without recalling how, in the year 19 A. D., the Emperor Tiberius had to forbid women of the aristocratic order to register themselves as prostitutes: a practice, says Sanger, which was "not uncommon." In point of fact, we know of only one Roman lady, Vistilia, who did this; and her action caused such sensation that her name lives in history. Further, although she registered as a prostitute for the same reason that lady-friends of mine went to prison in London a few years ago—to call attention to the vile position of woman in law—and we have no reason to think that she did more than merely register herself, she was sent into exile. And this virtuous incident is converted into a picture of crowds of "profligate ladies" surging to the brothels. The poet Juvenal tells us that the Empress Messalina did prostitute herself in common brothels, and his statement has become one of the classics of censorious literature. Not one writer in a hundred who repeats this seems to be aware that Messalina had been dead about sixty years when Juvenal wrote. All modern authorities warn us not to seek history in the picturesque and prurient satirist.

The worst disorders were seen under a few morbid and mentally unbalanced emperors whose reigns did not last long. Caligula was admittedly what a modern American calls, in the serious sense, a moron. It was he who set up a sort of brothel in the imperial palace and ordered maids and matrons of the aristocratic order to yield to the richest bidders, to help the imperial treasury. The alternative was death. The Romans slew him after a reign of four years. It was much the same under Nero, who was hounded to death in his thirty-first year. It is now widely admitted that he was not sane. At some of the gorgeous spectacles which he provided brothels were erected in which he compelled ladies as well as the professional prostitutes to give themselves to the mob, whom he wanted to conciliate. The city, says Tacitus, "teemed with funerals." The very florid picture of Roman life in the romance of Petronius belongs to the reign of Nero, when thousands of the best men and women were put to death because they had sober standards of life. And when the Romans had killed Nero, the empire enjoyed, apart from the few terrible years of Domitian, more than a hundred years of prosperous and admirable life. It is in these long periods under quite sane emperors that we find the true Rome: entirely naturalistic in regard to sex, with every caste of prostitutes flourishing, but with very little evidence of morbidity and overwhelming evidence of unselfish social beneficence. The early Romans died out, or perished in war, and the provincial blood that poured into the city maintained it for three generations in a generally temperate freedom. In the two generations before the fall the lower types of prostitution remained, as far as one can tell, much the same—the new religion, we shall see, made no difference— but the wealthy and nobles were more sober, even the "smart set," whose worst faults are described by Ammianus, not sinking anywhere near the old level.

CHAPTER VI.

THE TRANSITION TO THE DARK AGES

EFORE I describe how this large system of Greco-Roman prostitution fared in the revolutionary changes—religious, economic, and political—that now occurred, the reader will expect some account of the love life of the Asiatic civilizations. Unfortunately, as regards China, we have such small fragments of evidence relating to prostitution that we cannot describe it at this early date. Schlegel's *Historie de ca Prostitution en Chine* contains no history at all. It is a description of the situation in recent times which we will see later. He observed only that the Chinese "Holy Mother" is no goddess of love and therefore China never had temple prostitution. If I may apply my earlier figure, China entered history under the ensign of the sky-god. Heaven and the Will of Heaven were from the first, and until Buddhism and Taoism corrupted it, the essence of the Chinese religion. But the Chinese Heaven was no Ahura Mazda, frowning on the pleasures of mortals, and the sex-life ran its normal course. There seem to have been brothels from the earliest times, but the references to daughters of joy are very scanty, and we will assume that there was an extensive system, analogous to that of today, which the Confucian scholars disdained to notice in their writings.

Of prostitution in India, on the contrary, we have a very good knowledge, but, as I have said much on the subject in the **Story of Human Morals** (Vol. VII), it will be enough to interpolate a few observations here. Much misunderstanding has been caused by the saying of Mr. Havelock Ellis: "The English brought prostitution to India." When you read this in the distinguished author's own chapter on prostitution, you immediately find that it is just a rather careless paraphrase of the claim of some anti-British Hindu that, while of course there were shoals of temple-girls in India before the British came, it was they who introduced brothel-inmates as "the brutalized servants of the grosser desires." Havelock Ellis ought really to have turned down this nonsense with a smile. It is part of the reckless agitation of some of the young Hindu politicians, and it is a pity that our leading sexologist gave them so convenient a quotation. Long before the beginning of the Christian Era, and even before there were any temple dancers, India had one of the best organized and least despised bodies of prostitutes in the world.

Specialism has its drawbacks, and writers on sex and prostitution continue to repeat each other in regard to India in complete ignorance that our knowledge of its ancient history has been very greatly changed in recent years. They still write as if the Aryans had brought civilization to India, and they look to the Vedas for traces of some descent from a lofty primitive morality to prostitution. From the Vedas and the Laws of Manu we get very edifying statements about unchaste women, and we are told (as in the **Encyclopaedia of Religion and Ethics**) that the few references to harlots give us no clear idea of the extent of prostitution; that Buddhist literature shows an increase of prostitutes as well as royal harems; but that there is no clear evidence of extensive and organized prostitution until Mohammedan times. The general idea of Hindu history at the back of all this is quite false. We now know that the Aryan invaders, who were in the pastoral barbaric stage and therefore not likely to have prostitutes, entered an India that had already been civilized for more than a thousand years, and there is evidence that this early civilization had a cult of a goddess of love. In the light of these discoveries several Hindu writers have in recent years tried to trace in the Vedas the real life, about 1500 B. C., of the civilized people amongst whom the Aryans settled. Mr. Iyengar, for instance, in his **Life in Ancient India**, finds that prostitution already flourished when the invaders came. There are references to jewel-laden courtesans driving in chariots through the streets, and the general attitude toward sex is described as very free. Mr. S. C. Sarkar, another Hindu authority, gives us the same picture.

The references are naturally few and brief, but we have every reason to assume a steady growth of the system of prostitution until the time, about 300 B. C., when we get full light on it. I need not repeat the account given in the **Arthasatra**. There were three large classes of prostitutes attached to the court (apart from the king's harem), and their earnings swelled the royal treasury. A choice group of these ladies attended the king wherever he went. We are not told how numerous prostitutes were in the cities, but the writer, in describing the government supervision of them, suggests a very extensive body. They paid a tax of an average day's earnings once a month, and in the statutes they figured as a body of citizens of the same rank as musicians and hairdressers. India was at this time at the height of its civilization, and apparently prostitution was very prosperous and not at all despised.

There were then no bodies of dancing girls at the temples who prostituted themselves to visitors. It is the opinion of many experts that these began only in the ninth or tenth century of the Christian Era, when there was much temple-building and elaboration of the ritual. An inscription of the year 1004 A. D. shows that at one famous shrine there were four hundred "women of the temple." But the idea that "the brutalized servants of the grosser desires," or ordinary prostitutes, now ceased to exist, and all was sweet and beautiful until the wicked English came is fantastic. Long ago Sir H. M. Ellis gave from a contemporary Hindu treatise a description of prostitution in the city of Bijnagar in the fifteenth century (**History of India**, iv, iii). There is nothing quite so candid in Greek or Roman life. A bazaar three hundred yards long and beautifully decorated, in the center of the city, was reserved for the choicer ladies, and they sat, laden with jewels, at the doors of their exquisite houses, when the midday prayer was over, while their slaves invited men to enter. "The splendor of these houses, the beauty of the heart-ravishers, their blandishments and ogles, are beyond all description," says Sir H. M. Ellis. Unfortunately, he then remembers that he is English and says: "It is best to be brief on the matter." From the tax on these favored ladies and the supervised brothels of the city a force of 12,000 police was maintained! I repeat that India is the classic land of prostitution. The temple-system we will see later.

Let us meantime follow the development of the great area over which the Greco-Roman civilization had spread; and readers of my earlier works will not expect here the usual picture of a chaste transformation of the wicked pagan world into a garden of virtue. Sanger actually uses, as historical documents, such pure fiction as the legends of St. Agnes and other martyrs to show the vices of the Romans and the Christian repugnance to them. These writers, who take no trouble to collect references to prostitution after 380 A. D., are nevertheless embarrassed by one undisputed fact: every Christian emperor in the west maintained the tax on prostitutes as a source of revenue as long as the western Roman Empire existed, or for a period of a century and a half, and in the eastern or Greek Empire the tax was maintained by the Christian emperors for two centuries. For nearly a hundred years they continued also to draw revenue from the brothel-owners, whom all despised. A rich Roman offered, it is said, to indemnify the state if the very pious Emperor Theodosius would suppress the tax, but even he, though he abandoned the tax on brothel-owners, continued to levy it on prostitutes. In other words, though each emperor had a court of bishops and monks and bestowed enormous wealth on the Church, not one of them in more than two centuries abandoned the "tax on the wages of sin." At the best you may say that it was so important a part of the imperial revenue that to surrender it might be gravely embarrassing; but to say that this was true until after the year 500 is to say that prostitution was as prosperous as ever a century and a quarter after the establishment of Christianity.

In the Greek-Oriental half of the Empire, which suffered no catastrophe, prostitution continued unchanged. More than once we find the women intervening in the fierce theological tumults of the cities, and the Christian leaders give us the darkest pictures of vice in every part of the world. At last the Emperor Anastasius, an ex-peasant and lay preacher, decided to surrender the tax about two centuries after the conversion of Constantine. He did not begin to reign until 491. The Christian historian Evagrius tells with much satisfaction how it was done. Anastasius annulled the tax, burned the registers, and disbanded the large army of tax-gatherers and hunters of prostitutes. He then feared that documents still in the possession of discharged officials might be used later to restore the system. He announced—the lie does not in the least trouble the pious historian—that he repented his act, and he summoned the officials to search the kingdom for records from which he could reconstruct the register. When the collection was complete he burned the whole; though Evagrius does not say, as Sanger represents, that he called the people to the Circus to hear an announcement of the restoration of the register and burned the documents before them.

We must not for a moment suppose that this change was accompanied by any reduction of prostitution. Anastasius died in 518—he was succeeded by another peasant, Justin, with a peasant wife—and just at that time we have a remarkable document about the prostitutes of Constantinople. At the theater, which was significantly known (even officially) as The Harlots, the actresses, almost nude, were allowed to perform the most indecent gestures, such as mimicking the love-affairs of Jupiter, of the old Roman theater, and all were prostitutes. Amongst them was a girl in her teens, the future Empress Theodora, who surpassed all the others in her license on the stage and her share in nocturnal orgies with the wealthy young men. She was pre-eminent in both natural and unnatural vice and in every conceivable form of sex-pleasure. She practiced her profession, or professions, in every city of the Greek Christian world, became at last the mistress of the emperor's nephew Justinian, and in a few years "Theodora of the brothel," as a bishop-admirer simply entitles her in his work on the saints, was empress of the richest country in the world. It is always said in works on prostitution that Justinian altered the Roman law which forbade a noble to marry a prostitute; and we are asked to admire that act of mercy. But historians believe that he must have married Theodora before acceding to the throne, which seems to me certain, and therefore Justinian merely induced his peasant uncle to alter the law in order to make his union with the ex-prostitute a valid marriage.

The point of particular interest, which is usually ignored, is that the story very plainly shows that, nearly two centuries after the establishment of Christianity in the east, the system of prostitution and the general moral tone as regards sex were just the same as in pagan days. Theodora, it is said, then tried to bring about a reform. She had five hundred courtesans enclosed in a palatial "refuge" on the coast, but, in spite of all the luxury, a large number committed suicide, and the experiment totally failed.

The legislation of Justinian against procurers had no greater effect, and we continue from age to age to get glimpses of the unchanged maintenance of the system in the very sordid pages of Byzantine history. In the tenth century we again find an emperor choosing his mate, who turned out to be as sanguinary as Theodora and with no pretense of conversion to virtue, from the ranks of the prostitutes; and when, two centuries later, the Crusaders from the west sacked the churches of Constantinople, swarms of prostitutes are described as joining them in the debauch. In short, the Christian Greeks maintained and passed on to the Turks the very candid system of prostitution which they had inherited from the pagan Greeks.

We are more interested in what happened in Europe. The old type of historian, who saw prostitution, slavery, the games of the amphitheater, etc., passing away like clouds before the beneficent sun of the new religion, hardly exists today, and it is exasperating to find writers on the history of prostitution repeating his discredited statements. With very little trouble they would find that all these evils persisted in the eastern empire, where the Church was far richer and more powerful than in the west, and they might begin to suspect that, as every historian now sees, it was the political and economic ruin of the empire that wrought the changes in Europe. The population of Rome fell in two centuries from about a million to forty thousand: its wealth was even more terribly reduced. It was the same in most of the other cities, and it is therefore superfluous to say that the old Roman system of prostitution perished.

It is thus sheer waste of time to inquire into the supposed influence of Christianity on prostitution. Naturally the leaders of the Church in its purer days opposed it. St. Augustine, it is true, was already a Christian when, in his treatise On Order, he wrote: "Suppress prostitution, and you will bring about ruin." But Augustine soon came to share the common belief that all sexual pleasure was tainted, and that to seek it apart from the breeding of children was a crime. In the days, however, when the Christian body as a whole

followed this lead—until about 200 A. D.—it was far too small to
have the least influence on the Roman or Greek system of prostitution; and by the time when the Church secured influence and power,
it was itself deeply corrupt. I have shown all this elsewhere, but
the fact that no emperor abandoned the tax is eloquent enough.
Dufour, in his six-volume history of prostitution, makes a spirited
attempt to show otherwise. He fills four or five chapters with ficti-
tious material from the lives of the saints and martyrs, but he becomes gradually embarrassed when he has to tell of the new "sacred
virgins" sleeping with their spiritual brothers, of the vagabond and
dissolute monks, of the licentious love-feasts in churches, of nude
baptisms, and so on. When he reaches the real period of Church
influence he breaks down. He says:

> One does not find that the Councils attempted to do
> anything to eradicate prostitution from the civil life of
> Christian society. They seem, on the contrary, to have ac-
> cepted it as a necessary evil for the purpose of averting
> greater evils.

It appears that that plea is quite sound in a Christian mouth
but disreputable in a pagan. Dufour says that no gathering of bishops until the sixteenth century attempted to regulate the evil;
though I may say that a Spanish synod of the fourth century and
many later used some very strong language about brothel-owners,
and that the young Emperors Theodosius II and Valentinian III (as
dissolute a prince as ever there was) were induced to sign a futile
decree against them, while retaining the tax on prostitutes.

The Roman system naturally shrank with the disappearance of
Roman wealth, but the few references we have to prostitution in the
next few centuries show that wherever even a modest wealth was
again accumulated, the profession flourished. It is common to read
how the "hot blood" of the barbaric Teutons frustrated the work of
the Church, but it is precisely the barbaric princes who made some
effort to check prostitution. The first was the Vandal king Genseric,
who made fanatical efforts to destroy the system in Roman Africa,
where four generations of bishops had left it completely intact. But
the chaste Vandals were soon displaced by the Greek Catholics—
the Vandals were Unitarians—and the work was undone. Next
Theodoric the Goth, also a rebel against the Church, is vaguely described as making laws against "libertinage" in the cities of northern Italy. The third and most important case is that of the Gothic
king Reccared in Spain, near the end of the sixth century. As the
Goths were in a minority and the clergy very hostile to them, Reccared diplomatically embraced Catholicism and issued a decree
against prostitution. It is chiefly interesting as showing that wherever the new rulers maintained in some degree the old civilization,
prostitution was common. Spain, being the most sheltered province
in Europe, had now a prosperous civilization of an inferior type,
and its Church was very rich and powerful. But Reccared's decree,
the text of which is given in Rabutaux, shows that prostitutes were
numerous. Free women who adopted the profession were to have
three hundred strokes of the lash and, if they persisted, were to

become slaves. Female slaves who prostituted themselves were to be shaved and flogged. Women who roamed the streets and country were to be put in prison. Parents who prostituted their daughters were to receive a hundred strokes. A century later the Moors took over Spain, so we need not try to follow the development further.

Europe sank lower and lower, and there is scarcely any literature in which we may expect to find mention of social conditions. The chief work is the **History of the Franks** (of the sixth and seventh centuries) by Gregory of Tours, and there are few chronicles to equal it as a record of brutality and complete sexual license. Of formal prostitution we expect to find little trace, for money has disappeared, towns are few and small, every landowner has a gynecaeum of wife, concubines· and female slaves, and the mass of the people live, scattered over the land, in the most degraded conditions. The Franks, originally as chaste as the Vandals, had, Dufour deplores, converted the land into a brothel. Even in this half-barbaric world of the new Europe there must have been a good deal of the commoner sort of prostitution. In large numbers of the barbaric codes of laws we find drastic penalties imposed on the woman who calls another "a whore or a witch." In such towns as there were the moral tone can be gathered from the February festival or orgy which was taken over from the Romans and led in time to the Feast of Fools and the Carnival. In 743 the Synod of Hainault severely denounced this "Feast of Filth," as it called it. Men and women go about naked, imitate animals, and so on. One dimly sees a picture a shade worse, from the Christian viewpoint, than the old Floralia and Lupercalia.

Then at last, with the partial restoration of civilization by Charlemagne and the momentary appearance of some literature, we get a clearer view. Charlemagne is almost unintelligible to us, a monumental symbol of that strange age. He professed a zeal for religion but, in spite of all his monks and bishops, never for a moment allowed it to interfere with his robust amours. Yet we find him making the most desperate effort ever yet recorded in history to suppress prostitution. His decrees show that there were great numbers of prostitutes in his empire, but they seem quite early to have felt his antagonism and retired to hiding or to rural districts. They are to be sought out everywhere. The police must search the peasant's hut and the noble's palace. Every man who shelters one is to be flogged or imprisoned. There are, he says "many regions where the people are addicted to adultery, sodomy and intercourse with whores," and he has to forbid the priests to enter inns, which are still clearly temples of Venus as well as Bacchus, or to admit "strange women" to their houses. As Charlemagne's own court was what the preacher figuratively calls a brothel, his own daughters being as free in conduct as himself, his people did not respond very seriously to his call for purity. One finds until long afterwards a tradition in France that the "foot," as a measure of length, was standardized, not by Charlemagne's foot but another organ of his giant body. His legislation soon became a dead letter, and France, or the half of Europe which had been his empire, fell back into the condition which I described in the **Story of Human Morals.**

I will here carry the story as far as the twelfth century, when an extensive system of prostitution is found in every country of Europe. From 800 to 1100 A. D. we find only a few references to brothels, as when, in the year 1033, Pope Benedict IX complains that there is a brothel near the church of St. Nicholas at Rome, or when Bishop Liutprand tells us of the conduct of most of his brother bishops in Italy with courtesans. There is, in the first place, very little literature of that Dark Age in which we can expect to find details on the subject. There was, secondly, only a very feeble organization of the social and economic life. Money was rare, and towns were small. More than nine-tenths of the people were scattered agricultural workers, of whose life we shall see a little presently, and most of the small body of skilled workers were associated with an abbey or a bishopric. Further, apart from the clergy and monks, who monopolized the professions and arts, there was no middle class, and the life of the clergy, monks and nuns was, as I have amply shown elsewhere, so very free in the majority of cases that we may almost say that sacred prostitution was again established all over Europe. But the general attitude toward sex was so free and so completely devoid of refinement that we must suppose that a loose sort of prostitution was found everywhere.

It is hardly necessary here to recall the evidence. To all the evidence I have given elsewhere I might add such instances as the revenge of the wife of the Duke of Aquitaine, William IV, one of the great nobles of Europe, in the year 990. The Duke had looked with favor upon another noble dame, and his wife had her soldiers seize her rival as she traveled, take her into the castle, where they sexually assaulted her all night, and turn her out almost dead in the morning. Another noble of the age, making war upon his uncle and winning, threw his aunt to the ground before his soldiers and raped her. The princes and nobles, abbots and bishops, were, in short, so free and arbitrary in their conduct that they needed no professional women.

From the tenth century, moreover, there was such an epidemic of sodomy amongst them that this also must be taken into account. For some unexplained reason, this began with the Norman invaders of France. It is difficult to understand, because the Normans were almost the worst of the Teutonic invaders for raping the women and girls of the lands they overran. Yet the Norman knights were soon notorious in Europe for the practice of sodomy, which in large part involved male prostitution, and from Normandy the practice spread to the whole of France. The medieval historian of the Normans, Ordericus Vitalis, laments that "the effeminate [Sodomists] were paramount in every land." The contemporary poet Abbo, describing the seige of Paris by the Normans, says that the French were as bad as the Normans, and the Abbot of Clairvaux in 1177 wrote to Pope Alexander III: "Ancient Sodom rises again from its ashes." Naturally, the Norman nobles took the practice with them to England, and it was blatant in every castle. Speaking of the wreck of the White Ship in 1120, when the king's son and a body of nobles were drowned, the chronicler William of Nangis says that they were "nearly all tainted with sodomy." The Book of Gomorrah of Cardinal Peter Damian of the eleventh century teaches us that it infected the clergy all over Europe, and Cardinal de Vitry informs us that it was still so common in the thirteenth century at Paris that a priest who kept a concubine was deemed virtuous.

The student of these matters may care to be reminded again that this unnatural practice is no outcome of "oriental effeteness," but was epidemic in Europe in its most robust days, most particularly amongst the latest Teutonic warriors to issue from the forests of the north. The remaining evidence to which I turn shows that it was also widespread amongst the mass of the people, but I must confine myself to suggesting the general condition of sexual behavior and mentality out of which, when the economic conditions arose, came the remarkable system of prostitution of the later Middle Ages.

We have one set of documents in the Penitentials, or church books which assign the penances for various kinds of sin, and the lists of sins supplied to parish priests for the interrogation of their penitents. Any man who is familiar with these—few are, since we dare not translate the barbaric Latin—must smile at the customary reflections on Martial and Juvenal. These ecclesiastical documents describe far more varieties of sexual transgression than Martial ever knew, as well as all to which he does refer. The use of the mouth, sodomy, sapphism (especially in nunneries) . . . But I must refrain. I will venture only to say that apparently in every country of Europe during the robust Dark Ages, when there was no town-life to enervate people and very few knew even of the existence of Greeks or Persians, both sexes misconducted themselves with every type of domestic animal: nocturnal gatherings of women in the woods for the purpose of both sexual and homosexual orgies and with implements were common: women put menstrual blood and powdered testicles in their husband's beer, and men put seminal fluid and other matters in the drink of their wives. Church and state inflicted heavy punishments, and Dufour says that "the records of the Parlements [courts] are full of cases," but the ecclesiastical documents everywhere suggest that all these things were most common practices. It would open the eyes of many people if the police would permit us to publish in one volume a literal translation of the lists of sins of ancient Babylon, those of Martial and those of the Christian "civilization" of the early Middle Ages.

Dufour examines another class of evidence, but here one is even less free to put the full truth before a modern reader. He shows how during this period the French language acquired a vocabulary of sexual words and phrases of the grossest character. It was the same in every country of Europe. The general attitude was so naïve that ancient phallic deities became saints, and the sex-organs of saints were preserved and venerated in churches. The French had a legend of a St. Lenogesilus of the seventh century who was said to have lived all his time with a chaste virgin in his little cell. "Leno" is the Latin for brothel-keeper, and at that date was still in use as such everywhere. Every language in Europe was similarly enriched with words that one may not translate today. But in this respect Europe steadily became worse, and we shall see later how, in the most splendid period of mediæval civilization, the French language had more than eight hundred words and phrases for the sex-organs, the sexual act, and prostitutes. The grossest of these came into use in the period we are surveying. From some of these words we gather that prostitutes were commonly found round the wells, which were the chief nocturnal centers of love-life in every village, and that in some places they had houses on the bank of the river outside the village. The fact that legislation everywhere includes a penalty for calling a woman "a whore" confirms this, and the penalty was often itself a confirmation of our estimate of the time. Dufour reproduces an old picture of one of these penalties that was inflicted in a part of France. The guilty lady walks in her shift, which does not reach her knees, in the Sunday or feastday procession, and the injured lady follows with a bodkin, prodding her more fleshy parts. The Middle Ages roared boisterously over such things. We shall see many in the next chapter.

In sum, what we find between 500 and 1100 A. D. is just the same naturalistic attitude toward sex as amongst the mass of the people in the preceding Greco-Roman period. In particular, I would ask the reader to note carefully, the facts make a mockery of all references to "the nameless vices of the degenerate east." These millions of agricultural workers and soldiers in Europe, as robust as animals, who never saw even a town and learned nothing from cities, knew every practice in the sexual repertory. But this general freedom itself tends to make prostitution superfluous. The Greco-Roman idea of guarding the chastity of wives and daughters by having common women, for the most part foreign slaves, almost disappears in the Dark Ages. When we further recall the economic and social condition, that there were few towns of even twenty thousand people, few artisans, and no middle class, and that there is very little literature in which social conditions are described, we quite understand why we have only evidence of a brothel here and there. In such a world women would everywhere "prostitute" themselves for food or drink, as in the lower Roman world, or as women surrender themselves for drink in poorer quarters today, but we do not look for any traces of what one might call organized prostitution.

CHAPTER VII
THE AGE OF CATHEDRALS AND BROTHELS

SOME may suspect me of malice in the wording of the title of this chapter and may fancy that I strain the evidence for the purpose of outraging the conventional idea of the later Middle Ages. To these charges I should make an emphatic reply of not guilty. The age of the building of the beautiful cathedrals and abbey churches which still command the deep admiration of all of us is, in sober fact, the age in which Europe developed a system of prostitution as public and as carefully organized as that of any ancient civilization; a system that was, from the modern puritan's point of view, quite the most scandalous that ever existed. Men returned everywhere to the Greek and Roman principle: to guard the chastity of wives and daughters it was, whatever the Church taught, necessary to provide or tolerate brothels. During seven centuries after Charlemagne we find only two or three Christian princes who attempt to suppress this very conspicuous prostitution in their dominions. We find, on the other hand, great numbers of cities, princes, nobles (of both sexes), bishops (for some time even the Popes), and universities drawing revenue from them, and at times founding them, and quite generally protecting them. It is surely not malicious, but a very needed piece of historical education, to point out that the rich development of this system coincides with the evolution of the Gothic architecture, or medieval art generally, and the building of the great cathedrals.

Let me begin with a concrete instance: the development of prostitution in the city of London, or the city of Westminster which, though now a mere district in the large modern city, was in the early Middle Ages separated by a mile of country from London and was more important than it. In the year 1161, when not a stone of the present superb Westminster Abbey had been laid down, the Parliament of King Henry II passed a law for the regulation of brothels which you may still read, with interesting explanations, in Stow's *Survey of London*. The south side of the river Thames was at that time a disreputable and waste district to which the city authorities and the clergy relegated such entertainments of the citizens as were offensive to pious eyes. On the bank of the river, conspicuous to the eye of every child was a row of houses which were known as "the Stews." The name literally means "hot baths," and shows that the baths of France and Italy, from which the name came, were already mere brothels. Large signs were painted on the fronts of the houses, and amongst them were The Cardinal's Hat and the Cross Keys (the Papal coat of arms, or the keys to the kingdom of heaven). They were the recognized brothels of the cities of Westminster and London.

The Act of 1161 places certain restrictions on the owners. The "stew-holder," in the language of the Act, is forbidden to let women wander in and out at will, to provide board for them, or to charge them more than fourteen pence a week for the use of a room. The women, in other words, lived in Westminster or London, sought clients on the bridge or the river-bank, and took them to rooms they hired in the Stews. They were to close on holy-days and permit no single woman to enter them on such days. We rub our eyes when we read that the owners are further forbidden to admit nuns or married women or entice such to their houses. Laws are not passed to forbid what does not happen. Almost as naive a clause is this: "No single woman is to take money to lye with any man, except she lye with him all night, till the morrow." (Do not forget that the Parliament included the bishops and abbots.) The constables were to visit the stew-houses once a week and see that the rules were observed; and, as these constables were few and were busy in the city all the rest of the week, we can gather what usually happened.

How long before 1161 this state of things had existed we do not know, but Stow tells us of later developments. Let me say first that the Abbey began to rise in 1220 and building continued for the next two centuries. In this period the number of brothels increased to eighteen, and in the year 1380, we learn, they were owned (some say in the name of the city) by the Lord Mayor of London, Sir William Walworth, whom you will find described in the **Dictionary of National Biography** as a man of great piety and one of the most generous benefactors of the Church: it does not mention his brothels. His revenue came in part from certain "Froes of Flanders" (Flemish prostitutes) to whom he let the rooms: which suggests that there was already an international trade in prostitutes. Wat Tyler and his rebels, in their quarrel with Walworth, sacked his brothels. We find their privileges repeatedly confirmed by Parliament until 1506, when the severe Henry VII first attempted to close them and then, when it threatened to provoke a riot, reduced their number to twelve. Henry VIII, who was as virtuous as Charlemagne, sent trumpeters into the streets in 1546 to proclaim that they were suppressed. But a year or two later Bishop Latimer, preaching before the king, frankly said:

> Ye have but changed the place and not taken the whoredom away. I hear say there is such whoredom in England as never was seen the like . . . There is more open whoredom, more stewed whoredom, than ever was before.

We shall see that the bishop was right. Protestantism brought no change. But I must first give the facts for other countries during the second half of the Middle Ages, and they will confirm that the development of one of the most extensive and public systems of prostitution in history exactly coincides with the building of the great cathedrals in the thirteenth and fourteenth centuries.

The causes are so plain that the efforts of most modern writers, except the French, to conceal or mitigate the facts are quite absurd. The revival of art and the building of the great churches in Europe, which began in the twelfth century, were themselves, as I showed in **The Key to Culture**, consequences of the social and economic development: the growth and freedom of cities and the increase of trade and wealth. The same causes were bound to lead to a development of prostitution. They led also to a great expansion of school-life and the founding of universities, and this gave, we shall see, a powerful impetus to the growth of prostitution. Every attempt of a pious bishop or prince here and there to check the formidable movement broke down under the violent opposition of these hundreds, in some places thousands, of insolent and entirely undisciplined youths.

There were two other causes. One was the puritan movement in the Church, led by Hildebrand or Pope Gregory VII, which now imposed the condition of celibacy on the clergy: that is to say, declared their unions invalid and illegal. Most of them, and even some of the monks, had down to this time been married. We know well what their moral condition became and, though each had his female domestic staff, they largely patronized the brothels, baths,

and taverns (all different types of brothels), and the example of
their defiance of the Church code was not lost upon the laity.

A third and very important cause was the troubadour movement, or the spread all over Europe of a glorification, in defiance of
the Church code, of free sexual love. The character of the movement is, as I have shown elsewhere, now fully recognized. Dufour,
who wrote under the influence of the false older tradition about
chivalry, sets out to prove that it "purified prostitution." What we
may admit is that in the course of three centuries the troubadours
became more refined. A large number of the earlier songs, which
are reproduced with many dots and dashes by Emile de la Bedollière,
cannot be printed even in France today. But to the end they remained "the prophets of prostitution," as Dufour at last calls them,
and to the end many of the leaders were what a modern writer would
call very gross. François Villon, whose work is now much appreciated (though not literally translated), belongs to the fifteenth century. Jean le Meung, who completed the famous Romance of the
Rose (sexual love), is far more candid and erotic than the poet who
began it. The "shocking" poetry in which Horace and Catullus
glorify their Lesbias is refinement itself in comparison with a very
large part of the troubadour literature. One would almost say that
Europe, incited by the superb civilization of the Arabs in Spain and
Sicily, concluded that Paul's ban on the flesh was a tyrannical im-
posture and rushed to the opposite extreme.

A fourth cause that must be noted is the influence of the Cru-
sades. The way in which these developments are now described in
histories of the Middle Ages, without the least reference to the effect
on public morals, is deplorable and, in an age of education, gives
people totally false historical perspectives. The Crusaders were not
the first troops in Europe to have bodies of prostitutes in attendance on them, but it is significant that this kind of association is
almost first mentioned in connection with the Third Crusade. An
Arab historian, whose testimony is not questioned, says that when
the Crusaders were besieging St. Jean d' Acre in the year 1189, a
ship arrived from Europe bringing three hundred handsome women
for their pleasure. He remarks, rightly, that this was already a
custom in France. A French monastic chronicle records that in the
year 1180 fifteen hundred women followed the French army to every
country. From that time, at all events, swarms of prostitutes followed the armies in the innumerable wars. Louis IX of France—
St. Louis—complained bitterly that prostitutes abounded in the
camps in the Sixth Crusade. In the following centuries the practice
continued and grew. In the Chronicle of Modena we read that a
German commander of mercenaries (practically land-pirates), who
was ravaging the country with 3500 horse, had a thousand male and
female prostitutes with his men. In 1476 the Swiss troops won a
victory over Charles the Rash and found two thousand prostitutes
in his camp. Several of the Swiss cantons maintained prostitutes
to accompany their troops. Brantome tells us that when the pious
Alva took the field for Spain in the Netherlands, in the religious
war, he had with him four hundred prostitutes on horseback—and

they were "as beautiful and brave as princesses," the gallant chronicler adds—and a hundred on foot. Very few generals turned upon
them, but we read of one puritanical commander, the French Marshal Strozzi, who had eight hundred prostitutes, who persisted in
following his army, thrown into the Loire. So Varillas states in his
authoritative History of Henry III; and it is curious to learn from
the article on Strozzi in Bayle's Dictionary that the marshal was
a pronounced skeptic in religion.

These movements of medieval life fall exactly in the period of
cathedral-building, and it is generally an unpleasant subservience to
religious untruth that prevents historians from describing both sides
of medieval life. When these same historians pompously assure us
that American psychology has enabled us at last to understand the
"real spirit of the Middle Ages," we wonder to what depths the
teaching of history is descending. They ought to know that this
rapid growth of prostitution in Europe becomes plain to us in the
chronicles just after the supposed purification of the morals of the
Church by Gregory VII and the stricter monks, on which they lay
much stress, and before any of the Gothic cathedrals were built. I
have shown this in the case of England and will now show that
it is true in every country of Europe.

It is particularly true of Paris, the center of the development
of the cathedral architecture, and one does not wonder that those
monuments of the ages of faith, the great churches, had to be purified of most erotic and licentious carvings on their walls when France
passed into its skeptical phase. In my Story of Human Morals
I described the extraordinary freedom that spread over France in
the eleventh century—"lust and shameful pleasure were openly ram-
pant," says the Catholic historian of the Church of Paris—but
said little about prostitutes, unless one cares to include under that
head the priets' servants, almost all mistresses, who changed from
master to master, and the nuns, who were, Abélard and Heloise
assure us, for the most part corrupt and complaisant to the laity.
But we have ample traces of prostitutes and brothels before the end
of the eleventh century. Paris was still a small city, and Abélard
had not yet attracted scholars in their thousands to its school, but
clearly it had so many prostitutes that everybody was familiar with
them. Abélard himself professes that before his connection with
Heloise he had "ever abhorred the uncleanness of harlots." The
charge of an abbot of the time, that Abélard lost his fortune through
"the greed and avarice of harlots," is false, but it shows that prostitution flourished at the time; and it was so leniently regarded that
in later and quite ascetic years we find Abélard, in spite of the severe
language I have quoted, advising his son that "a humble harlot is
better than she who is chaste and proud."

The system is more plainly described by the twelfth-century
historian Cardinal Jacques de Vitry, a severe monk; though we must
remember that by this time the brilliance of Abélard had converted
the body of a few hundred students at Paris into several thousand.
De Vitry, who knew Paris well, says that the clerics (mainly clerical
students, no doubt) "saw no sin in simple fornication," and "the

more freely they spent their money in vice, the more they were
commended and regarded by almost everybody as fine, liberal fel-
lows." The ground floor beneath a school was often a brothel, and
"common harlots were to be seen dragging to their brothels the
clerics who passed by." The women accused men who declined to
go with them of sodomy, which was still very common. Sauval
says in his **Antiquities of Paris** that the prostitutes had their own
guild, statutes, patron saint (Mary of Magdala, of course), festivals,
and processions, like the other workers. He gives no evidence of
this, and Dufour suggests that it was cut out of his work. The
students were the champions of the women against every effort of
reformers to check them. Whether or no the prostitutes were already confined to certain streets—De Vitry does not suggest this—
as in later years, there must have been a great body of independent
prostitutes who hung about the meadows where the students played
and fought, the woods round Paris (which was then not a mile in
diameter), and especially a ruined Roman building nearby which
was notorious for its crowds of lovers. The system grew in just the
same period as the beautiful cathedral of Notre Dame was rising
on the island in the river.

Many references could be quoted to confirm this extensive development of open prostitution before the end of the twelfth century.
In the year 1176, we read, a French princess gave the customary
kiss of peace to an elegantly dressed lady whom she met at the
church. She afterwards discovered, and complained bitterly to the
king, that the young woman was "a harlot of the court," in the
words of the chronicler, and we must suppose that a prosperous
class of prostitutes followed the court to its various residences. In
1190 the famous preacher Fulques de Neuilly began to preach in a
wood near the gates of Paris where the youths of Paris used to
meet prostitutes of the homeless type. He is said to have converted
so many of the women that a convent was built to accommodate
them; and Dufour maliciously tells us that for six years the "converted" prostitutes and "converted" male followers of them were
housed together in this place by the simple preacher. In 1198 we
read of two other preachers of Paris who opened a mission to con-
vert prostitutes. "The sinners came in crowds," we are told, and
many were converted. In point of fact, attendance at church, with
conspicuous rosary beads and other pious decorations, was a recognized way of attracting men. We must remember that at this date
all were staunch Catholics and witnessed with joy the burning of a
heretic. In the year 1220, in fine, the Chronicle of the monks of St.
Denis complains that there are on the roads everywhere prostitutes
of the vagabond or cheapest type.

About the middle of the thirteenth century France had for
monarch a canonized saint, Louis IX, and he naturally fell with
great severity upon the thousands of prostitutes in his kingdom. By
imposing heavy fines and confiscation of all possessions—he drew
the line only at the lady's underclothes—he attempted to suppress
the entire system. The women, naturally, retired from the cities to
the country and the roads along which thousands of students trav-

eled, and such complaints of disorder reached the king that he had
to surrender. He then ordered that the women must confine themselves to a dozen streets outside the walls, and that it was to be
considered a mark of degradation for any citizen to be seen in those
streets. He lived to enforce his laws for thirteen years, and his
successor is said also to have enforced them. But we are familiar
with the actual working of such experiments, and we are not surprised to find that within a generation the general moral condition
was worse than ever. Three sisters of the king—the Queen of
Navarre, the Countess of Poitiers, and the Countess de la Marche,
all married—were put on trial for extraordinary debauchery and.
found guilty. They used to watch the students and invite the more
handsome and robust to their chateau or tower, and, after the pleasure, they had the students murdered so that they should tell no one.

There are two ways of writing the history of prostitution in
France at this period. One is to tell how year after year the authorities passed decrees for the purpose of checking the women, and the
clergy made protests against sexual vice. Some writers confine
themselves to this pleasant task, and they thus give the reader the
impression that while prostitution certainly existed, Church and
State and the majority of the citizens sternly opposed it. But this
restrictive legislation has little significance. The municipality of
Paris did not, like so many others, derive a revenue from brothels,
and its authorities could the more easily be induced to compel the
women to retire to the streets appointed for them, from which they
were constantly invading other quarters. This restriction to certain
quarters became a very general practice in European towns, and in
very many—we are not sure about Paris—a prostitute had to wear a
distinguishing mark (an epaulette, a colored cap, and so on) so that
she should be recognized if she wandered from her quarter. But
there was amongst the citizens no shyness in regard to the brothel
quarters. The streets often bore names that we should today not
be at liberty to translate. In the city of Blois there is still, or there
was in the nineteenth century, a street called the Rue Pousse-Pesnil.
I must not .reproduce some of the others even in French. Thirty
years ago during a long stay in Nice I made some research into the
meaning of the peculiar name of an important street. It was the
name of a medieval prostitute who was said to have saved the town
against Saracen or Turk besiegers by jumping on to the ramparts
and exposing her person to them ; whereupon, the legend says, they
fled. Such stories were boisterously appreciated in the Middle Ages.

It was natural that at times the really religious minority should
insist on the observance of the existing laws about prostitutes and
get them confined to their quarters, but the attempt was not always
successful. All through the fourteenth and fifteenth centuries there
were at Paris struggles of this type, and several times the prostitutes, who seem to have had their attorneys, won. In 1386 a bishop
found that brothels were creeping up to the very walls of his garden,
and he appealed to the king, but the women succeeded in holding
their ground in spite of bishop and king. In the following year
some of the citizens moved against the women, and the great lawyers

of the Parlement upheld the claim of the prostitutes. In another struggle, in which the women lost, it is recorded that the canons (probably canons regular, a semi-monastic body of priests) owned the brothels and fought for the women. But these dates and details are of little consequence. No one questions that the body of women continued to grow during the great period of universities and of cathedral-building, and it will be enough to give a general picture of the situation at the close of this period or in the fifteenth century.

It is clear, in the first place, that there were still elegant prostitutes who depended on the royal court and followed it from palace to palace. Dufour says that they were subsidized from the royal purse. One of the officers of the royal household was entitled "The King of the Wantons" (Ribauds), and it is generally agreed that he was the superintendent of the court-prostitutes. Neither he nor they lived in the palace or its dependencies, and his position in the king's household was low. The Dukes of Normandy and Burgundy, who were then independent princes, had similar officials in their households, and, as we shall see, several important cities appointed Kings of the Prostitutes in imitation of the royal example.

In Paris itself each brothel-quarter chose its own "king" (in some cases queen), generally an elderly and sedate man who conducted his business as gravely as a funeral-furnisher. In these recognized quarters there were—if we may anticipate a clerical estimate of a somewhat later date—about six thousand prostitutes: at least, this figure cannot possibly include the lowest types which I will describe presently. Sometimes the quarter, if it were in a pleasant district by the river, bore some such title as "The Valley of Love" or "The Garden of Roses," but most of the recognized streets were squalid and disorderly. One was called the Street of Hell. Very few streets of Paris at that time were either paved or lit at night, and the noise in the evening was one of the chief reasons why citizens objected. One must not imagine men in medieval towns slinking quietly, in the dark, to the brothels. Crowds enlivened the quarter with their drinking, singing, and fighting.

In the more elegant quarters there were, as at Athens and Rome, beautiful and expensive women. Sumptuary laws were repeatedly passed to prevent them from wearing silks and furs and jewels, or the gilt-leather belts which the Crusaders had introduced from the east, but they were not consistently enforced. The function of the women in the life of the community was so far recognized that a creditor had to count access to them on the part of his debtor one of the necessities of life. On festivals they marched soberly under their own banner of St. Mary Magdalen or St. Mary of Egypt (a converted prostitute to whom they built a chapel), and on such bacchanalian holidays as the Feast of Fools, when religion was indecently parodied even in the cathedral, they mixed turbulently with the citizens. Their liberty, naturally, varied with the mood of the reigning monarch and prelates. Under Louis XI they expected, and received, such license that when, in 1461, he entered Paris in state, three of the most beautiful courtesans sat completely nude at one window; and it was "a very pleasant sight," says the chronicler.

The troubadours spread the fame of the more beautiful all over the city and the country and defiantly sang the praises of the free life of the prostitute world.

But these inmates of the recognized brothel-quarters were only a minority of the entire body of prostitutes. The school quarter, on the hill outside the walls where the Latin Quarter and the Boule' Mich' are today, is said by the French experts to have contained mere prostitutes than there were in all the remainder of the city. Naturally it was a world of taverns or wineshops, and each seems to have been in effect a brothel. The Golden Cat and four or five other large taverns openly enjoyed that repute. But there were also numbers of brothels, and there were swarms of homeless women who plied their cheap trade in the vineyards, gardens, woods and fields. At this time there were probably about ten thousand students. The impressive account which you often read of the grave Scholastic theologians lecturing to crowds in the schools gives quite a wrong side of the medieval university world. It was a world of the wildest license. More than once the students fought the governor of Paris and his troops; and one governor, who had (probably for just cause) hanged a few students, was compelled by the king to go with his councillors to the gibbets and kiss the corpses. Above all the students fought for the liberty of their women and taverns. Even the barbers, we learn from city edicts, took part in the trade.

Besides these there were prostitutes of the cheaper or older type in the woods and fields round Paris on every side, and the apprentices and soldiers especially went out to them. Although it now had perhaps quarter of a million citizens, Paris was still a small, heavily walled city, and quarter of an hour's walk anywhere brought you to the woods and vineyards (which then flourished round Paris). But I will be content to describe a peculiar branch of the profession which was as squalid as any type of prostitution in the older civilizations. In the foulest parts of the city, approached by dark and narrow winding streets, were what men called the Courts of Miracles: so called because when the troops of blind and lame and maimed beggars turned in at night, their wounds miraculously disappeared, to reappear the next morning. Thieves and criminals mingled with them, and at night the quarter was a hell. Here were the lowest types of prostitutes, who charged from two to ten cents: while the average of a decent courtesan in the recognized quarters was four dollars a day. The more handsome boys and girls born in the quarter were trained as outside prostitutes, using every art to attract citizens to the Court. A man would find a pretty girl weeping at a corner, or she would accidentally collide with him, and so on. If he went to the Court with her, he was lucky to come out alive and almost nude.

I have dwelt at some length on the situation at Paris, partly because we have good contemporary evidence and a large number of modern French works, but mainly because most writers on prostitution give a full account of it in ancient Athens and Rome and almost ignore the equally candid system of the medieval cities. I dislike generalities which cannot be supported by statistics, but I should say that the men of medieval Paris who took the Pauline view of these matters were not more numerous than the men of Athens or Rome who frowned on prostitution. Certainly the majority regarded the sex-life of the town as freely and gaily as had the majority in Athens or Rome. The clergy and stricter officials had generally to be content to take action against procurers: who, we saw, were despised in Greece and Rome. We read of quite a number of cases at Paris in which procurers were branded with a hot iron or had their ears cut off, or procuresses (they were generally women) who were pilloried and banished. In 1399 the officers of the Bishop of Paris oiled and set afire the hair of one of these women. This kind of savagery was, however, comparatively rare, and the poets seriously counteracted the efforts of the puritans. It was not until the religious struggle began in the second part of the sixteenth century that there was a drastic attempt to suppress prostitution at Paris. We shall see later what happened.

It is just as great an error to suppose that the conditions of city-life at Paris had brought about there a license of thought and conduct which was unknown in the rest of France. On the contrary, what we read about sex-life even in small country towns is often more ingenuous than life at Paris. There are French writers who hold that, just as it was the rural Normans who infected Paris with sodomy, so it was the southern provinces, which were more exposed to Moorish influence, that led in the development of this free attitude of the later Middle Ages. As we have already seen how prostitution was found in abundance far north of Paris when the rule of Charlemagne led to a temporary growth of wealth and literature, we should distrust this. The conditions which I described at the beginning of this chapter led to the same development of prostitution and free views about sex all over Europe. Practically everywhere, until some pious prince or fanatical bishop got power —and they were rare— the principle was accepted that, whatever the theory of the Church was, prostitution was an indispensable means of preserving in some degree the chastity of wives and daughters. We shall see an amazingly frank acceptance of it in the smallest towns. But I will devote a separate chapter to the French provinces and the remainder of Europe.

CHAPTER VIII

PROSTITUTION IN MEDIEVAL EUROPE

IF we were to make a comparison of morals in Christian France and pagan Rome in the loose and not quite honest fashion in which moralists and religious writers make that comparison, yet with a strict attention to all the known facts, we should find that France was immeasurably looser in sex-matters than ancient Rome. Of the number of prostitutes we have just one estimate in the case of each capital: 6000 at Paris about the year 1500 A. D. and 32,000 at Rome in the days of Trajan. Such figures are of little value, but we have a right to assume that they are of the same value in each case, or that something like the same proportion of women in each case are not included in the police estimate. And since the population of ancient Rome was four or five times that of the population of Paris in the year 1500—since Rome had no "celibate" nuns (the Vestal Virgins numbering only a score or so), monks and priests, but had immense numbers of foreigners and at least quarter of a million adult male slaves—we cannot say that, from our present angle, the old pagan city was worse than medieval Paris. To that point the comparison is fairly just.

But, as I said, we could, if we follow the usual practice, make out a large balance of virtue on the side of the Romans by including the provincial cities and towns in the comparison. For the Roman Empire we know almost nothing of prostitution (in Europe) outside of the metropolis: in the case of medieval France we have abundant proofs of the existence of organized prostitution in every large town and much prostitution in the smaller towns and country generally. Although at the period I am covering there were only three universities, at Paris, Toulouse and Montpellier, there were very important schools in many cities. The students moved, generally afoot, all over the country, and great numbers of prostitutes followed their tracks. Apart from the students and soldiers, indeed, every town adopted the current maxim that prostitution must be tolerated to avert greater evils. We therefore find brothels in every large town, and we have a surprising number of references to the temporary sojourn of prostitutes, who wandered over the country, in very small towns or large villages. The evidence I shall give in this chapter is an incomplete account of the state of France, from our present viewpoint, in the later Middle Ages. These are instances which French scholars have brought to light from medieval archives and official registers. There has been no approach to a complete search. Yet before the end of this chapter the reader will probably agree with me that they suggest a more extensive and candid system of prostitution than is described anywhere else in literature; and you will not forget that we are still in the great age of cathedral-building.

I am not in the habit of misleading my readers by these loose comparisons, and I will repeat my warning that absence of facts may mean simply absence of documents that describe them. Even with this condition the medieval situation impresses us as, seeing that other countries were in much the same condition as France, far beyond what we find today in any civilized land or have reason to suspect in the ancient civilizations. The medieval French language confirms this impression. We earlier found some of our historians of prostitution declaring that there was "unparalleled" vice in Rome because Martial describes acts and uses words which have no parallel. The first point I have settled: the Middle Ages knew more about sex than Martial or Juvenal did. The second point must seem ridiculous to any man who has read Rabelais, or Sir Thomas Urquhart's literal translation of Rabelais, which gives equivalents in late medieval English for the appalling terms and phrases of the French. A French authority on Rabelais, a priest, the Abbé de l'Aulnaye, published in 1820 a glossary of "Erotic Words" culled

from Rabelais and other French sources. From this and similar
lists we learn that in the age of the beautiful cathedrals, the friars,
and the early universities the French language had three hundred
words or phrases to express the sex-act, four hundred different words
for the sex-organs, and more than a hundred words for prostitute!
The Latin and Greek languages are poor in comparison. Even
Greek had only fifty words for the sex-act. The reason is not only
the entire frankness of the general attitude toward sex—there is a
note of joy in all these lists—but that the wandering prostitutes and
troubadours picked their words out of dozens of different dialects in
different parts of France and even from the Spanish and Italian
languages.

There is no doubt that much of this elaboration of the language
of love, if we may use that expression—a very large number of the
words are very crude—occurred at first in the south of France. We
are, of course, at once reminded that the Albigensian heresy spread
over the whole of this region, and we are left to infer that it was
responsible. I might retort that the Albigensian heresy included a
quite Pauline contempt of the flesh, since the "elect" were forbidden
to marry, but I will say at once that the great body of the heretics
took no more notice of this than Christians took of the message of
the gospels. On the other hand, we saw, the Normans spread their
own looseness over France before the heresy had captured Provence.
The truth is that from the twelfth century onward the same causes,
which I have given, led to a great development of prostitution in all
parts of civilized Europe, and they were particularly operative in the
rich and industrious towns of southern France. Probably also the
nearness of the Moorish civilization counted there, for the region
was certainly one of the cradles of the troubadour movement. However, the evidence I am going to give refers in nearly every case to
the southern cities long after the Albigensian heresy was drowned
in blood, and it shows just the same state of affairs in northern cities.

Toulouse was the metropolitan city of the south, and the story
of prostitution there is interesting. We trace a brothel there in the
twelfth century under the Counts of Toulouse, and at the beginning
of the thirteenth century the Albigensians were destroyed. What
happened to prostitution in pious Toulouse? The university and
the municipality maintained the chief brothel and divided its revenue
between them. By a supreme irony it was called, even in official
documents, "the Great Abbey"; as if to invite a comparison with the
character of abbeys of nuns. It was outside the city walls, and the
girls were compelled to wear, when they went abroad, white hats
with blue cords on them. In 1339 the French king, visiting the city,
listened very respectfully to their complaints of this ignominy, but
there was no change until 1424, when for some reason the youths of
the city began to break the windows and burn the doors of the
brothel. The women began to leave, and the university and
municipal authorities, seeing the loss of revenue, tried in vain to
check the disorders and then appealed to the king. We have the
text of the royal letter in which the king rebukes the students. I
have read it and can assure the reader that it is quite true that the

king charges the students with being "wanting in the fear of God" (non verentes Deum, in the Latin text) when they attack brothels. The royal banner was floated over the brothel, to protect it, but the disorders continued, and the municipal authorities—the university retired—set up a brothel for the women in the town. There they plied their trade, to the profit of the civic treasury, for a century and a half. It was no pressure of the Reformation that put an end to the Grand Abbey. In 1559 four of the prostitutes were found in a neighboring monastery and were hanged: in 1566 three were discovered in another monastery and hanged. The scandals shook the magistrates, especially as citizens accused them of buying their fine robes out of the profit, and it was offered to the hospital, on condition that the doctors treated the prostitutes and those they infected. Syphilis was now rife, and the doctors refused; and, in short, the singular brothel was suppressed (as a source of infection) in 1588, and the work was left to private enterprise.

At the old university city of Montpellier the brothel was from early times private property. Early in the fifteenth century a banker joined the enterprise with his capital, and a handsome building, with baths and fine furniture, was opened. The city granted the owners, for an annual payment, a monopoly of their trade in Toulouse. When a rival defied the monopoly and set up a brothel, the owners appealed to the king, and they got a royal privilege or confirmation of their monopoly. In the other cities of the south there was invariably some form of prostitution. At Narbonne the police had no jurisdiction over the women. At Sisteron the brothel had to pay its annual tax to a community of nuns. At Nimes a special magistrate was appointed to control the affairs of the prostitutes. At Beaucaire, where there was no resident bishop, the lady superintendent of the brothel was officially entitled the Abbess, which implies that the building was known as the Abbey, and the municipal statutes gravely laid it down that she must not sleep with the same man on two consecutive nights, or she must pay a fine. One lady-abbess paid the fine six times. Every town in the south had its brothel, generally under municipal control.

But the same system prevailed nearly all over France. At Rouen, which was then in the possession of the English, there was a public brothel, with a Marshal as supervisor, and it was the same at Bordeaux. At Provins and Angers (which had famous schools) the prostitutes were highly praised by the troubadours for their charm and beauty. At Avignon the long residence of the Papal Court drew crowds of prostitutes, as Petrarch describes, and, in spite of decrees which seem severe when you read them, the women sought clients at the doors of churches and even of the papal palace. In short, we trace brothels or prostitutes in every city and often in towns which are otherwise unknown in history. We find that in 1283 the tax on the prostitutes at Verneuil, a small town, went to the king, so that it cannot have been a trifle. In very many places, which cannot have been much above the rank of villages, the local lord or lady taxed every prostitute that came in the pursuit of her profession. In the fourteenth century we find a noble complaining in a letter to the widow of the Duc d'Orléans (the king's brother) that his income from this source has gone down by one half.

The freedom of French writers for the last fifty years to tell the truth about the Middle Ages and the Church has led to a great deal of research of this description in medieval archives and chronicles, and the result is extraordinary. From princes and cities to local landowners we find a quite general custom of taxing brothels or traveling prostitutes. There is in no country today the slightest approach to the picturesque condition of medieval France. Where the local lord or lady was rich and indifferent to the levying of a few coins on any prostitute who came to spend a few weeks in the village, an official took the tax, sometimes in kind. We have legal documents laying down that this or that lord of the manor is entitled to a small sum of money "or something else." I will give only one instance, and it throws an extraordinary light on the frivolity in this respect of the medieval folk. Dufour reproduces the Latin text of the charter of the noble lady of Breuil, a very small town, Margaret of Montluçon. It makes the surprising stipulation that every prostitute who comes to Breuil must either pay three cents to the lady's treasury or—how shall I translate it?—be taken to the drawbridge of the castle and there, lifting her skirts, make a certain very rude noise ("unum bombum sive vulgarites fret," if you happen to understand medieval Latin and French). We may be quite certain that this would take place when the people were idle and there would be a roar of Rabelaisian laughter, the great lady and her family looking on from the battlements. Such were the men and women who built the cathedrals of Chartres, Amiens and Rheims.

We have not such ample information about other countries, though all the evidence we have suggests that this was the general condition of medieval Christian Europe. For Germany, fortunately, several historians have made extensive research in this respect, and we shall find a system in many ways as far removed from our time as that of the French. But let me first speak of Strassburg, which the French and Germans both claim, though it is an essentially German city. In the Middle Ages, at all events, it was far removed from any taint of Norman vice, Provençal heresy, or Moorish luxury, yet we find prostitution as prosperous and unashamed in Strassburg and Metz as in any city of the south. The women, who had to wear black and white conical hats (which encouraged the men and youths to greet them in the streets with boisterous and indelicate jokes) were confined by law to certain streets, and these bore such expressive names as Klappergasse, etc. But seven times in the course of the fifteenth century the city authorities had to check their expansion beyond these limits. Procurers and brothel-owners brought girls from all countries, and they would more justly be called "white slaves" than the daughters of joy of Rio and Buenos Aires.

The public brothels, one of which had been founded by the Bishop of Strassburg, were taxed, so that the police kept a vigilant eye upon pirate or non-paying establishments, yet at the end of the fifteenth century they had to report to the magistrates that there were a hundred in the city, fifty-seven of them being found in six short streets. The girls from these, "the swallows," as the good burghers genially called them, so openly sought customers in the cathedral and the other churches that the city council had in 1521, when the shadow of Luther was falling upon this gay world, to issue a formal decree expelling "the swallows or cathedral girls" from the sacred buildings. So free was the general mood that we still have the account-book of an important city official, who enters: "For . . . . . 30 pennies." For the missing word supply the grossest English term for the sex-act. Whether it was Luther or Syphilis that put an end to this gaiety in the next few decades we will consider later, but the historians assure us that the women merely passed from brothels to inns and baths and barbers' shops, to private rooms and dark corners of the city.

For Germany generally Rudeck has brought together a most valuable and exactly documented body of facts in his History of Public Morals in Germany and I have checked his statements and derived some additional evidence from Max Bauer's more recent work. Both these are works of scholarship and authority, yet the general picture which they conjure up would otherwise, as in the case of France, seem quite incredible. Apart from one or two vague early mentions of brothels, we find a rapid growth in the thirteenth century: Augsburg 1273, Vienna 1278, Hamburg 1292, Basle 1293, and so on. This thirteenth century, which is selected by Catholic writers as the fairest in history, was essentially the century of brothel-building, and I have explained why any man of common sense will expect this. The evidence I am going to quote will show the system spread over the whole Germanic region from the thirteenth to the sixteenth century, from Hamburg and Dantzig to Geneva, Lucerne and Vienna; from Cologne to Berlin. The brothels were commonly owned by the princes (even prince-bishops and archbishops) or the city councils, and the women in very many cities received civic honors and mingled with the highest burghers in a way to which there is no parallel in history. Except in early India, as I described, or in Papal Rome at the height of the Renaissance, I know no period in which, over a vast area, prostitutes became such a recognized feature of public life as they did in Catholic Germany.

Let me at once tell of certain disabilities which seem to contradict this, but which must be understood in the light of what we shall see presently. Some authors quote for you cases in which procurers or even prostitutes who broke the rules were publicly branded or scourged, or had their noses cut off; but these cases are rare, and there is in most of them the weakness that the city owned brothels and was severe on private enterprise. It is, however, quite true that the children of prostitutes were greatly despised—in most places to call a man "son of a ——" was heavily punished, yet it seems to have been significantly common—and nearly everywhere the women, when out of doors, had to wear a distinguishing mark. In the majority of cases it was a short yellow cloak, sometimes with blue facings. At Lubeck they wore black bands on their arms, at

Vienna a strip of yellow cloth on their shoulders. At Basle they wore red cloaks, and at Berne and Zurich red caps. As loosely flowing hair was a mark of maidenhood, they had always to wear a veil (sometimes with green stripes), a cap, or a hood. In many places they were forbidden to wear velvet or gold out of doors. Everywhere, in fine, a city refused to allow girls or women (except in certain cases of delinquency) of that city to become prostitutes, though they might come from a neighboring city.

On the other hand, we find instances of freedom and even civic prestige which are not found elsewhere in history, and they range all over Germany. When the Emperor Sigismund, accompanied by eight hundred horse, spent a few days at Berne in 1414, the city fathers informed the managers of the brothels that they would pay all fees of Sigismund and his men, and in a public speech the Emperor thanked the magistrates for their generosity. Twenty years later Sigismund visited Ulm, and the municipality illuminated and decorated the streets leading to the brothels for the convenience of the emperor and his officers. When he visited Vienna in 1435 the city fathers clothed all the women of the public brothels in velvet and sent them, with the notabilities, to meet him. You may know that Emperor Sigismund (the gentleman who purified the Papacy and burned John Hus) was exceptionally amorous. It is recorded that he was awakened in bed one morning by a few courtesans, and he flung on a few clothes and went out to dance with them in the street. But there are many other instances. When Albrecht II came to Vienna after his coronation, the city council sent the prostitutes to meet him and, as the archives still show, regaled them with wine. In 1452 the prostitutes were conspicuous amongst the crowd of ladies sent to welcome King Ladislas. When Frederic III was at Nuremberg in 1471 two prostitutes met him on the street, flung a silver chain over him, and said, "Your Grace is a prisoner." He laughed and ransomed himself with a gold coin. When he passed the brothel four other prostitutes held him to ransom, and he responded with the same generosity. When Charles V entered Antwerp in 1520 there were in the group of welcoming notabilities a number of the more handsome prostitutes, and the flowers with which alone they were clothed did not conceal much. "It was thought," says Rudeck, "that no greater pleasure could be given to princes than to give them free entry to the brothels."

Lest it be thought that these are just concessions to the taste of vulgar monarchs, let me say that it was a common custom to put women from the city brothels at the disposal of any guests of distinction, and that in many other ways the representatives of the chief citizens showed a most remarkable familiarity with their public women. The German tongue had, like the French, many ugly names for prostitutes, but it is significant that, while the common name in early French official documents is "foolish women," the common German expression is "beautiful women." The account books of the city of Vienna of the fifteenth century show that the corporation often paid for "beautiful women" for its distinguished guests. In 1493 we find Count Eberhard of Württemberg writing

to the city fathers of Ulm, his capital, that his advanced age prevents him from attending their civic dinner, but he sends game which
they are to eat with the "beautiful women." A legal deed of the
year 1544 tells us that the Dean of the Cathedral of Würtzburg was
entitled to receive every year from the village of Martinsheim, on
November 12th, a horse, a meal, and a beautiful woman. A deed of
1498 tells that every year the Counts of Castell had to give Götz von
Berlichingen, Goethe's hero, a meal and a handsome woman.

At Vienna and several other cities the women took part in the
races which took place on one of the chief festivals, and at Vienna,
on St. John's Eve, they danced round the great bonfire, and the
council provided refreshments for them. At Nürnberg the women
were, until 1496 (when syphilis begins), invited to the dances in the
civic hall. At Altenburg they were, until the sixteenth century,
invited to the civic banquets. At Frankfort they attended the annual civic banquet until 1529, the city fathers providing a banquet
for them in their brothel after that date. In very many cities they
used to attend rich weddings and receive presents for their good
wishes. At Magdeburg in the thirteenth century we read of a
"beautiful woman" as the prize in the races of the rich young men,
and elsewhere we find one as the prize in a shooting contest. At
Würtzburg the city fathers had a luxurious and boisterous banquet
in the brothel with the prostitutes on St. John's Eve. The general
attitude toward them was so human that we find, in 1446, an envoy
who was sent by the Frankfort Council to Cologne including the
cost of a visit to the brothel in his official list of expenses, and the
archives of many cities often name their choicer prostitutes—"Else
with the long teats" occurs in the Berlin archives—as if they were
a matter of civic pride. Quite commonly they were, since they came
from other cities or countries, officially granted the rights of citizenship, "to encourage them to cooperate in the prosperity of the city,"
as the magistrates of Nürnberg put it.

There are innumerable other evidences of the benevolent attitude of the city fathers, which clearly means that the great majority
of the people regarded prostitution leniently, if not with positive
approval. Here is a passage from the contemporary Chronicle of
Nuremberg by Heinrich Deichsler. It appears that in 1492 the
women of the public brothel had presented to the mayor a long list
of independent prostitutes and had asked, "in the name of God and
of justice," the historian says, that they be punished. Whether they
were or were not checked, they again increased, and this is what
happened on November 26th, 1500:

> On this day eight common women from the common
> brothel came to the mayor, Marchart Mendel, and said that
> there was a house full of whores; that the mistress of it ad-
> mitted married men to one room and bachelors to another,
> day and night, for the purpose of lust. So they asked per-
> mission to storm the house and destroy it. The mayor
> gave permission; and they took the house by storm, burst
> in the doors and broke the windows, each one carrying

something away. The birds had flown, but the mistress was there, and she was cruelly beaten.

They did the same again, without asking permission, in 1538; and this time they carried off the girls to their own brothel. The women of this city and very many others formed a guild like all other workers, and they were empowered to sue in court any girls who practiced prostitution and did not belong to the corporation. At Biberach the head of the brothel had to present a horse to the city every year. At Würtzburg he had to take an oath "to be loyal to the city and protect the women." At Geneva the magistrate chose a "queen," and she in the name of the others took the oath of civic loyalty and was much respected. At Ulm the head of the brothel had to swear at the civic hall to "maintain fourteen healthy, clean and suitable women." At Leipzig, where there were four great colleges, and the public brothel was popularly known as the Fifth College, there was on the night before Lent began a "Procession of Whores," as everybody called it. Between double ranks of citizens the prostitutes of the city walked, two by two, in procession through the streets, singing songs which seem to have been a defiance of death! The leader bore a straw man on the top of a pole, and, when they threw this into the river, the people believed that the service of these pristesses of love preserved the city from plague during the ensuing year.

Nor were these civic authorities who owned or protected brothels always laymen. I have told how the Bishop of Strassburg founded a house, and we find in legal documents of the year 1457 that the Archbishop of Mainz drew part of his income from a tax on prostitutes. At Frankfort the municipal authorities hired their three brothel-buildings from three different bodies of monks, including the Carmelites and Dominicans, and paid rent to them; and a deed of the year 1388 shows that the brothel at Beedbuch belonged to the monks. Fees were generally small, as money then had a high purchasing value, but in so free and stimulating an atmosphere the clients would be very numerous. We actually have a civic ordinance of the city of Ulm of the year 1527, the time of Luther, which forbids the women to admit boys of twelve, thirteen and fourteen to the brothels, and it is the only place where we find even this restriction. Jews, on the other hand, were excluded, as intercourse with them was understood to taint the Christian prostitute; and the brothels were closed on Sundays and holy-days, when the ladies all attended church.

I must add a few particulars about the public baths, partly because they were everywhere notorious haunts of prostitutes, partly because they both reflected and encouraged the general naturalism as regards sex. From a very early age baths, hot in winter and cold in summer, were very popular in Germany. For the hot baths there were single or double tubs, and quite commonly a man and a woman occupied the double tub. Numbers of engravings show these establishments, a dozen or more tubs under one roof, generally with open sides, often with a musician to entertain the bathers. Mixed bathing was denounced in the Penitentials, quite uselessly, as early as the ninth century, and in the thirteenth and fourteenth centuries, when there were baths in almost every village, it was general. Only in a few places, especially in the north, do we read of a separation of the sexes, and this would be effected merely by a wooden barrier that did not prevent each seeing the other. Artists like Dürer used to make their studies of the nude at such places.

I have elsewhere shown how familiar these medieval folk were with the nude form from their infancy. Bauer says that until the second half of the sixteenth century all Germans—nobles, burghers, and peasants—except monks and nuns, slept nude. One has to be careful in reading medieval statements of this kind, as "nude" often means in the chronicles that a man or woman has only a shirt on. However, as in the overwhelming majority of families adults and children slept in one room, as there was only one open dormitory at the inns and even the wealthier sometimes slept ten or a dozen in a large bed, there was not the least feeling of delicacy about exposure. When the bath-heater blew his horn, men and women ran almost nude, the children up to the age of seventeen or so quite nude, along the streets to the bath. For the poorer folk there was a common undressing room for both sexes. In any case, they generally bathed nude, and without any enclosure or privacy. Female servants, who were commonly prostitutes, assisted even the men. Not until the middle of the sixteenth century do we find decrees separating the sexes, ordering that all shall keep on their shirts until they enter the bath, and prescribing male attendants for men; and by that time syphilis had swept over Europe, and the baths were in decay. This applies also to the open-air tank-baths which, as I described in the **Key to Love and Sex**, drew as many as a hundred thousand people to some cities during the summer. Here some clothing was generally enforced, but conduct was of the freest kind. Men and women, priests and laymen, even monks and nuns, played gaily in the shallow water, and there was usually a retiring room or a brothel close at hand.

Such was life during what are called the ages of faith in the entire Germanic area, from the Baltic to the Adriatic, from Belgium to Bohemia. Since Russia, though now Christian, lay outside the pale of civilization, the Balkan lands were subject to the Turks, and the best part of Spain belonged to the Moors, it will be understood that this account of prostitution in France and the German Empire covers the greater part of civilized Europe. The record is scanty for other countries, but I can add a little about England that has been overlooked by all other writers on the history of prostitution. London was still, at the end of the sixteenth century, a small city with a population of about 100,000, or one-fourth that of Paris, so that one does not expect an extensive system. But the common assumption that the citizens of London and Westminster were still content with the row of stew-houses on the disreputable south side of the river is quite wrong. Civic documents inform us that the ale-houses of the city, which were very numerous, were centers of prostitution, but we have very much clearer evidence in the records of the Ecclesiastical Courts, from which copious selections are given in Archdeacon Hale's **Series of Precedents and Proceedings in Criminal Cases.** I have related or translated most of these in Little Blue Book No. 1550 (**How People Lived in the Middle Ages**). Twenty-five of these cases belong to the middle of the fifteenth century, the remainder being selected at dates in the next half century. Half of the whole are sex delinquencies (adultery by priests, exposure and obscene language by drunken priests, incest, etc.), and brothels are frequently mentioned. Several married couples, living in the city, are summoned for keeping brothels, and all that they are asked to do is to deny it. Women are accused of being "common whores" or procuresses. One married couple ran a brothel for monks and priests, the wife being one of the prostitutes, while the girls drag in friars and priests from the street. One man seduces servants and sells them to the brothels on the Stew-side. One girl is a "common whore" for the clergy, sometimes in church, of most notorious practices, yet she is not even summoned. In short, "whore" and "bawd" occur on every page, and it is clear that all these offenders belong to London proper, not to the Stew-side, where prostitution was legal. The broad picture of London life is, especially when we bear in mind that there were no police seeking out cases, one of quite general unlicensed prostitution. One reads with amusement in Traill's **Social England** that the country cannot have been wholly corrupt at this time as it was "instinct with vast animal life, robust health, and muscular energy." These moralists cannot shake off their precious theory of a necessary connection between decay and sexual looseness.

We do well to notice also that if it were not for this rare book of Archdeacon Hale's, and we had only the few references to brothels which are usually given, we should have a totally false idea of prostitution in England in the later Middle Ages. We may apply this caution to Spain, for which also the evidence is scanty. Rabutaux reproduces from an ancient work one of the most singular accounts of prostitution apart from Hindu literature. A French traveler visited the city of Valencia in 1501, and he wrote with enthusiasm of its civic brothel. It was "as large as a small town and enclosed by walls, with a gate," at which a most courteous porter received the guests. Inside there were three or four streets of small houses, scrupulously clean and elegantly furnished. In these houses there lived between two and three hundred dainty prostitutes dressed in satins and velvets. A wineshop, a cabaret, and other places of entertainment were included in the colony, and the city sent two doctors to examine the girls every week. We shall see later that we must recognize the refining influence of the Moors in this southern city, and that other cities of south Spain had similar arrangements. But for Spain generally we have only a series of royal decrees against prostitutes and procurers. From 1575 (after the introduction of syphilis, note) to 1623 we have a large number of these decrees. Public brothels are suppressed, prostitutes are forbidden to have carriages or litters, to wear silk and jewelry, and so on. A suggestive peculiarity is that Spanish prostitutes are repeatedly forbidden to wear the costume of nuns or to use handkerchiefs in church. But all these ordinances merely show the futility of the struggle. In a decree of the year 1611 Alfonso IX distinguishes his five classes of procurers: men who procure girls for brothels, men who keep women in their own houses, men who buy slaves or young girls, men who prostitute their wives, and men who hire their rooms to prostitutes. Clearly there was as much prostitution in Spain as elsewhere, and fanaticism merely made it more furtive.

Italy I defer to the next chapter, since it is chiefly interesting in connection with the Renaissance. I close this section on the Middle Ages with two pertinent observations. One is that, in any attempt at comparison with antiquity, we must remember that there were forms of medieval looseness which did not exist in the older civilizations, and they relieved the need of prostitution. One, of course, is the corruption of the clergy and monks. Of every million adult males something like 50,000 were priests or monks, and they quite generally had concubine-servants or relations with nuns. Further, there was, especially amongst the mass of the people, not so high a standard of chastity of wives and daughters in the Middle Ages as in Athens or Rome. Finally, there was the witch-movement, of which I have written fully elsewhere. These nocturnal meetings of women, and some men, in the forests for the purpose of orgies, are already mentioned in the Capitularies of Charlemagne in the eighth century. They developed very rapidly and became a most extensive secret organization after the puritan movement of the twelfth century.

The second point is that we must not be misled by the formidable laws against procurers which figure largely in histories of prostitution. At Paris in the fourteenth and fifteenth centuries procurers were open to a sentence of branding, ear-cutting, and exile; and we find cases in which the ears of men were cut off and the hair of women was oiled and fired. Yet Paris continued to have an ample supply of prostitutes. In some parts of France the procurer was taken through the town on a horse or an ass, a word which the French writers will not translate for us being written large on a placard they bore. At Naples they might lose their noses, under one king their lives. In the Duchy of Aosta the man or woman was taken round the town, preceded by a trumpeter, in a cart loaded with ordure, while the people pelted the victim with filth. At various times, in most cities, from Geneva to Bruges, we find them flogged, branded, mutilated, imprisoned, banished or put to death. It sounds very virtuous, but the fact remains that all Europe during this period had as extensive a system of prostitution as ever existed, and procurers must have been very numerous. The city of Lucerne had in 1529 *three* hundred prostitutes to four thousand people. The ecclesiastical Council of Constance in 1415 attracted a thousand prostitutes. Public brothels were supplied in hundreds of cities. Large as the collection of decrees against procurers is, we can see in it little more than expressions of puritan anger which were rarely enforced.

CHAPTER IX

THE RENAISSANCE PERIOD

BEFORE we pass from the Middle Ages we ought to glance at prostitution in the Arab-Persian kingdoms in which civilization had taken refuge. Unfortunately there is very little documentary evidence, and we are thus deprived of a study of the profession in an atmosphere that must have been more favorable to it than any other. Mohammed sought to meet the sex-life of his male followers by the concession of the harem, but I have shown elsewhere how little notice the more brilliant areas of the Arab-Persian civilization took of the restrictions of the Koran. In Syria, Spain, and Sicily, even in Persia and Egypt, wine, which the prophet sternly forbade, was more familiar than drinking water to millions, and love-poems and songs were as ardently cultivated as among the troubadours. We may assume that the general liberty of life included a great deal of picturesque prostitution, and the tales of the **Arabian Nights** often confirm our assumption. But I must refrain from taking pictures from fiction, and our standard authorities on the Moorish or the Arab civilization tell us so little on this point that it would be merely misleading to quote it. Doubtless life was much as we find it in the Mohammedan world today, though immeasurably more refined, and we will study that later. In the next chapter we shall get some idea of Moorish arrangements from the Spaniards.

It is acknowledged that the Moors and Saracens inspired the amorous troubadour movement in Europe, but, as we saw, the development of the brothel-system of the Middle Ages proceeded from different causes. We saw that system beginning, mainly on account of the growth of schools and cities, in the twelfth century, and in most countries we found it expanding, until the first quarter of the sixteenth century, in exact proportion to the growth of wealth and cities. The reader will therefore now be prepared to find that the influence of the Renaissance upon the sex-morals of Europe is generally greatly exaggerated. The fiction is sustained by ignoring the mass of evidence regarding medieval prostitution which I have given and thus persuading the reader that it was the revival of the wicked pagan literature that corrupted the virtue of the Middle Ages. I have elsewhere given a piquant illustration of the absurdity of this, and I may briefly recall it. In the year 1416, when Greek and Latin literature was confined to a few scholars and had not yet a wide influence, one of its most immoral and most ardent apostles, Poggio Bracciolini, a Papal secretary, author of the most advanced collection of erotic stories that was ever written, visited Baden. I imagine that the extraordinary gathering of German prostitutes which he had just seen at the Council of Constance had provoked his curiosity. Now, one may or may not hold that Poggio had been perverted by Greek or Latin literature (though both are predominantly moral), but the point is that he wrote to his

Italian friends that the life of the bathing towns of Germany, where the Renaissance was unknown, was far freer and more joyous in regard to sex than it was in Italy. We have a long letter in which this decided expert declares that Germany is surprisingly franker in sexual behavior than Italy.

It is therefore entirely false that the Renaissance led, through Italy, to a greater laxity of sex-morals in Europe. I have carried the story of prostitution in France, Germany and England as far as the beginning of the sixteenth century, and we saw that there then was in each a complete development of prostitution and a quite general naturalistic attitude toward sex matters. But at this time, say the year 1500 A. D., the classical revival had not yet had the least influence outside Italy. In Italy itself the situation was peculiar. The cities of north Italy, which were more advanced in civilization than Rome, were in the thirteenth century for the most part included in the German (or Roman) Empire, and through Frederic II they had felt the influence of Saracen life in Sicily. Before the classical revival began there was in them a general sexual freedom, and there was a great deal of sodomy. From Peter Damian's **Book of Gomorrah** to Dante's poem the evidence is consistent; and the peculiarities of the moral judgment of the Catholic poet himself, who in defiance of theology puts sexual sins amongst the less serious, are informing. Two centuries later the sermons of Savonarola present just the same picture. There is no dispute about the enormous prevalence of sexual license in north Italy, as I have shown in the **Story of Human Morals.** The one point on which serious historians claim an influence of the Renaissance is an apparent increase of sodomy, but it is really an increase of literary men, especially poets, who write about it.

The earliest Norman kings of Sicily had attempted to check the sexual freedom which south Italy had cultivated under its Saracen rulers, but within a generation or two the Normans adopted the free spirit of the Saracens, and there was a great development of prostitution in Naples and Palermo. It will be understood that Frederic II did not restrain it. He, on the contrary, removed some of the disabilities under which the women suffered. By the fifteenth century the system was as conspicuous as in the rest of Europe. One sometimes reads of a statute of the year 1470 which forbade innkeepers to give the women credit. But this was in the interest of the women themselves, for men used to compel them, under threat, to take over the credit of their drinks, and this put the prostitutes in the power of the publicans. It is useless to quote the attempts of Spanish rulers to check the system. They did not restrict prostitution, but they led to much hypocrisy and injustice. The special court appointed to take cases against prostitutes degenerated into the familiar practices: batches of women were periodically arrested, and those who paid the officials were set free. By the year 1500 the women invaded the finest quarters of Naples, such as the Square of Toledo, where the nobles lived, and both there and in the quarters of popular entertainment the trade was plied openly and noisily. All this had developed steadily from the thirteenth century, and it was not affected by the Renaissance, which led rather to greater laxity on the part of maids and matrons. It was only in the last quarter of the sixteenth century that rigorous measures were taken, and by that time syphilis, which the French called the "Neapolitan Disease," had disturbed prostitution all over Europe.

The cities of north Italy were for the most part included in the German Empire, and therefore to the freedom they adopted from Germany was added the influence of the south when Frederic II inherited the Empire. As a rule, they confined the women to particular quarters of the city and compelled them to show distinguishing marks when they quitted those quarters. At Mantua and several other places the brothels were civic property. We know little about them beyond the restrictive laws that were passed, and these seem at first sight to reveal a quite puritanical spirit. At Milan the laws imposed a public flogging or a period in the galleys for venturing into the respectable quarters of the city in daylight and other offenses. At Pavia the public crier every six months ordered all thieves, prostitutes and heretics to leave the city. At Mantua the women had to wear a white cloak and to carry, like lepers, a little bell, and they were sternly forbidden to mix with respectable women. At Parma also they had white cloaks: at Padua red hats: at Bergamo small bells on their caps. These rules imposed no restraint on the growth of prostitution, as the cities became rich, and by the end of the fifteenth century they were commonly disregarded. At Milan, where the laws were most severe, the women were found in some of the best hotels and, indeed, all over the city. In these Italian cities bastards were not even a joke in the fifteenth century, and the sexual attitude throughout Italy was as free as in any period of history. Venice developed a system of prostitution that became famous throughout Europe, and it was so little affected by either religious or political changes that three hundred years later we find Casanova, who was a Venetian, remarking on nearly every page that the more elaborate kisses and caresses of his innumerable mistresses were "really Venetian." The magistrates set up a brothel and invited elegant foreign prostitutes to it, in 1421: to preserve the virtue of their youths (from sodomy) and women, they said. A grave matron was put in control, and the general attitude of the citizens was as candid as in Germany. The women formed a union of their own. The baths, also, were nearly always brothels, as an Italian writer of the sixteenth century, Garzoni, assures us. He ascribes this character to them in nearly every city of Italy.

The city of the Popes had not been subject either to Saracens or Germans, and the development of prostitution there deserves special consideration. Rome lagged behind all the other great cities of Italy in the recovery of civilization, and the removal of the Popes to Avignon in 1309, where they remained for seventy years, left the city beggared and unprogressive. It is often represented that the Popes returned to Rome, or at least peacefully settled in it once more, just at the time when the Renaissance was perverting morals, and that we must take account of this in judging the undisputed demoralization of the city in the fifteenth and early sixteenth cen-

tury. On the contrary, Avignon under the Popes had a very liberal
and extensive system of prostitution and, though the city remained
Papal property (with the surrounding country), it and the neighboring cities developed one of the most ingenuous systems of prostitution in Europe. It was from Avignon that the Popes brought to
Rome the practice of taxing prostitutes for the benefit of the Papal
treasury.

We have in the case of the city of Avignon one of those valuable works, based upon thorough research in the local archives, which
suggest to every thoughtful person, that, if the same research were
made in the medieval archives all over Europe, our history of prostitution would be very considerably enlarged. In the work in question Dr. Le Pileur collects the original documents from the thirteenth century to the seventeenth. Before the Popes arrive we find
Avignon a sleepy little city of the usual type. Brothels are tolerated, but the prostitutes must never mingle with respectable women
and must not even touch food that is exposed for sale in the market.
The deeds of the next century, when the Popes reside there, reflect
that extreme license which Petrarch so indignantly describes in his
letters. We learn that brothels are opened near the doors of the
churches and of the Pope's palace. These deeds fully confirm the
fact that the Pope's marshal or lay governor of the city levied a tax
on the prostitutes, for the Papal treasury, and the only restraint was
that brothels must not be opened near churches, and the women
must not flaunt their silks and jewels in the street. One document
is amusing. The pietists of the town have angrily destroyed a
bench in one of the churches which the prostitutes had monopolized.
The Pope's officer takes the puritans to court, and they are compelled to provide a new bench for the ladies!

In 1421 we find that the brothels are repaired at the expense
of the city, and the vagabond prostitutes (who compete against the
Papal brothels) are forbidden to sleep more than one night in
Avignon. We next find that an official announcement is issued
that a "fine and respectable new brothel" has been opened by the
city, and the Pope's subjects are in effect invited to patronize it.
It is true that priests are forbidden to go to it—rather, the officials
try to stop their practice of going to it—and the girls are forbidden
to drag men to it on the streets or snatch their hats to compel them.
Within ten years, the archives show, two more new brothels are
opened in Avignon, and one of these is near the Franciscan monastery, while the third is in premises rented from the abbess of a
nunnery. In another document we learn that the city-fathers, the
Pope's local representatives, have bought a brothel from a doctor's
widow, and this long and solemn deed opens with the words: "In
the name of Our Lord Jesus Christ. Amen." At last the terrible
new disease appears in the archives, and after 1550 the brothels are
"suppressed." Simultaneously, we may note, cases of sodomy, infanticide and prostitution of daughters by parents make their appearance, and unauthorized brothels, of which twelve are counted in 1689,
multiply.

Dr. Le Pileur has made the same research in the archives of

neighboring towns that were under Papal rule or under the influence of Avignon. At Besançon in 1468 we find that there are twenty-five women in the public brothel, and they pay, collectively, about sixty dollars (then worth four or five times that sum) to the treasury. At Nimes the manager of the public brothel is entitled Abbess in the official documents, and she presents a gold ring yearly to the Consuls. In another official document the Abbess is called the **maquarelle**, which is the vulgar name for "procuress," and she receives civic gifts at the church door. At Tarascon a document shows the sub-vicar of the parish purchasing, in legal form, the revenue of a brothel.

These facts, taken from a work of indisputable scholarship which reproduces the deeds and decrees, though I fear you will not find them noticed in any other English work, show the utter hypocrisy of all apologies for the Popes. During more than a hundred years before any one of them took the least interest in the classical revival they all drew revenue from prostitution and protected it in their own city. And this singular practice of levying a tax on "the wages of sin" they transferred to Rome and maintained it there for nearly two centuries. The contemporary historian Infessura tells us how the French were scandalized to find the Papal officials still levying the tax on prostitutes in 1557. Burckhardt, the leading authority on the Renaissance, tells us that at one time in the fifteenth century, when Rome was the richest city in the world, the Papal Treasury derived twenty thousand ducats (about $50,000, but in modern value quarter of a million) from prostitution. This was under the "pious" Franciscan Pope, Sixtus IV. At that time, Infessura says, the officials counted 6800 prostitutes at Rome, not including the obscurer and poorer women. Rome had become the rival of Venice and Naples in every variety of prostitution.

The profound corruption of the Church and the Papal Court which explains this development I have described elsewhere. Writers who try to dismiss it with a blushing allusion to the sins of Pope Alexander VI trifle with history. In the quite orthodox Rinaldi's **Annales Ecclesiastia** (XXX, 152) we read that Pope Pius II (a defiant apostle of free love until he was seized with clerical ambition) issued a decree forbidding priests to own butcheries, wineshops or brothels, or to take money from prostitutes to get customers for them. This was about 1460, thirty years before the accession of Alexander. But the scandal grew, and Pope Innocent VIII renewed the decree quarter of a century later. In his notes to Burckhardt's **Diary** the distinguished French scholar Thuasne says that apparently Pope Innocent repented of his severity, for when in 1490 his Vicar issued an edict forbidding the priests to have mistresses, he cancelled the edict, remarking that "scarcely a priest or official of the Curia can be found who has not a concubine or at least a prostitute, to the praise of God and the Christian Church." Let me explain that neither Sixtus IV nor Innocent VIII took any interest in the Renaissance or read classical literature, yet it was precisely under them that prostitution became more blatant at Rome than in any other city of Europe.

I say that the system was "more blatant."—a phrase which is surely justified when one reflects that Rome was the heart of a religion that sternly forbade fornication and that most of the prostitutes derived their income from Church money—not merely because the head of Christendom, through his lay officers, drew more money from it than any other city did, but because at Rome, and almost at Rome alone, there developed a body of courtesans similar to the looser hetairai of ancient Athens. The Athenian ladies provoke the disgust of moralists because, we are told, they show that the moral sense was perverted even amongst the most cultivated and refined of the Greeks. The hetairai of Athens were certainly more numerous than those of medieval Rome but, as we saw, until a late date they were not, as a body, prostitutes. At Rome the score or more whose names have come down to us, the more beautiful or accomplished members of a large body, were all prostitutes, though at times they became the mistresses of cardinals or nobles. Foreign ambassadors visited them and gravely reported their arrivals and departures in their official dispatches. Cardinals, bishops, princes, poets and scholars pressed to their splendid palaces, as artists and statesmen had once gathered at the house of Aspasia, who was not a prostitute. "You would take them for duchesses," a contemporary said. Pilgrims to the holy places at Rome, says Rodocanachi in a special work on them, hastened to get a sight of them, the second wonder of Rome, as soon as they had visited St. Peter's, for they were famous throughout Europe. They were of all countries— Spanish, English, French, Flemings, even Greeks and Syrians—yet their testimony in a Roman court was as good as that of a noble, and they sat at the banquets of the rich with the finest ladies of Rome and the daughters of the Popes. Their palaces vied with those of bankers and cardinals in the elegance of the furniture and the choiceness of the wines, and even the less conspicuous of them rented the finest apartments in Rome. One of the latter, Panta, spent more than a million dollars in a few years. Another, Tortera, had with her, when she went out, six elegant gentlemen and six servants. Michael Angelo wrote a poem on one of them; and it was reported by the Mantuan ambassador that at a feast given by Cardinal Serra there were as many Spanish courtesans as Italian guests. At official ceremonies they stood in the sanctuary, near the prelates, and when they died they often had superb monuments in the churches.

These women all lived by their sexual services, whatever accomplishments they had. One of the richest, the Spanish beauty Isabella de Luna, did not even make a profession of refinement. Her sexual vocabulary and her stories were such that she boasted that she could make any man blush yet would not blush herself. Very different was the Spaniard Tullia d'Aragona: "a sweet lady, so reserved, so seductive in manner, that one feels there is something divine about her," says a contemporary writer. She was not beautiful but an accomplished musician, a brilliant conversationalist, a woman of the finest taste in jewels and furniture, an esteemed friend of ambassadors, prelates and nobles; and the sole source of her income was prostitution. From rich Germans she got fees of $250 for a visit; and she died a pauper. Even more accomplished was the Italian courtesan Imperia, "the most noble whore of Rome," said Alexander VI, the greatest lady in Rome under Pope Julius II. Her library was as choice as the vases in her golden boudoir, to which only the elite of city and Church were admitted. The story ran that one day the Spanish ambassador, in the crowd in her salon, spat in the face of a servant, explaining that in so beautiful a room he must choose that spot. One version is that the salon was so crowded that he could not spit on the floor. And all Rome wept when "the young Phryne" died at the age of twenty-six; and she was buried with great pomp in the church of St. Gregoria, with the epitaph:

> Imperia, Roman courtesan, who was worthy of so high a name and whose body had a beauty that is rare amongst mortals.

Her daughter committed suicide rather than yield to the solicitation of Cardinal Petrucci. There were others, who knew every line of Petrarch and Boccaccio and a good deal of the Latin poets. Camilla of Pisa also had a splendid library, and her rooms were decorated by one of the leading painters; and she said, when she had to give evidence in court about a serious brawl in her rooms one night, that next morning she had visited six churches—to meet clients. There was Beatrice, who specialized in entertaining clerics; Laurona, who sought merchants; Madrema, the favorite of the nobles; Francesca of Venice, who dined with Pope Leo X and her banker lover Chigi . . .

These and a hundred others were the most famous women of Rome from the middle of the fifteenth to the middle of the sixteenth century; and there were others in the cities of north Italy. Apart from the Isabellas, who relied on beauty alone, they helped to refine Italy, and here we can certainly admit the effect of the Renaissance. The historian of Rome, Gregorovius, says that Beccadelli's saying, that prostitutes were more useful to the world than nuns, was now generally accepted, and the lack of cultivated women in Roman society gave an opportunity, as at Athens, to the more accomplished courtesans. The "sense of sin," which moralists deplore in the ancient civilizations, was a rare thing in Rome. A few preachers thundered hell at the crowd of prostitutes in their audience, and we read of fifty or a hundred being converted together. But even conversion seems to have been strange in that world, for we read of one converted prostitute who resolved to enter a convent and, when a lover met and persuaded her at the last moment, she said: "Well, hurry up, they are going to make a nun of me." It was very largely in church that they met and negotiated with men. Bunches of men gathered at the doors and bowed to them as they entered and left.

But a few details from one of the most authoritative books of the time will give a good idea of the candor of the age. This is the Diary (in Latin) of Johann Burchard, Master of Ceremonies at the Vatican under three Popes, who certainly did not write for publication. Describing an important ceremony, with seven cardinals present, in a church in 1497, he grumbles:

> All was in disorder. Prostitutes and other common folk stood about everywhere, even between the altar and the cardinals [that is to say, in the sanctuary].

In the next year, he notes, a certain "courtesan" (cortegiana, originally a lady of the court, now the Latin and Italian for the more elegant prostitutes) or "decent prostitute" (as distinguished from the "whores" or "candle-girls" of the dark corners) has been arrested. Cusetta went too far even for Rome. She had a negro servant, and she dressed him as a girl, called him Barbara, and made money by his sodomy. But listen to the quaint way in which the virtue of Rome expresses itself. He is taken through the streets of the city holding his female skirts "above his navel, so that all can see his genitals and recognize his fraud"; and a man riding on an ass in front of him bears on the top of a pole the testicles of a Jew who has been so shameless as to have relations with a Christian prostitute. This is in the heart of the period of cathedral-building and superb art at Rome.

But let us get on. In 1501, Burchard notes, the French have arrived outside Rome, and the Pope has sent to the French commanders wine and choice food and "sixteen prostitutes to meet their requirements." On the last Sunday of October of the same year the Pope has not appeared at vespers, as he ought to have done, but he has a banquet in his rooms in the Vatican with his son Cesare Borgia and his daughter Lucrezia and "fifty decent prostitutes." After supper the women dance naked with the male servants of the Vatican. Then chestnuts are scattered over the floor and candles put on it, and the Pope and his son and daughter watch the bending and dancing of the nude women as they pick up the nuts. The last phase is so extraordinary that Catholics try to impugn the veracity of Burchard: on the quaint ground that, in such a world, he liked naughty stories. The Pope gave rich prizes to the courtesans and servants who, in his presence in the open room, had intercourse the largest number of times. But the fact is confirmed in other documents of the time, as the editor of the Diary, Thuasne, shows One ambassador tells his government that twenty-five or more of these "decent prostitutes" are admitted to the Vatican night after night. In another entry Burchard tells us that the Roman prostitutes take part in the races at the end of the year, and that on one occasion Cesare Borgia, a cardinal, and the Pope's secretary have been absent from Rome in a ship with two "beautiful courtesans" for three weeks.

These were the select few of the 6800 prostitutes who were known to the Papal officials at that time; and beyond those would be more thousands of women who, as in ancient Rome, served the soldiers and workers in taverns or squalid rooms, in the dark streets or the open spaces. This state of things had developed, as I said, more than half a century earlier, or as soon as the Papal court was firmly established at Rome after the Great Schism. Most writers are content to tell how Pope Julius II—they do not add that his own record is appalling—assigned a special quarter for prostitutes (the rule was certainly not observed); that Leo X (who was even more immoral) regulated their conduct; and that Clement VII (a bastard) ordered them to leave half their property to a nunnery—a provision which their lawyers defeated for them. But they do not tell how in 1525 the Pope's misconduct led to such a sack of Rome by the Spanish and German army that the population was reduced from 90,000 to 32,000, and, in modern money, several hundred million dollars worth of loot were taken away. It was even worse than syphilis, which had raged amongst the prostitutes for twenty years: it was one of the worst ravages in the history of Rome. I have described it in my **True Story of the Roman Catholic Church** and shown how it affected the culture and morals of Rome. The city was terribly impoverished, the higher types of courtesans passed to the cities of north Italy, and it was easier for the Popes to proceed against the common women. "What a poor Jubilee it will be," says a Roman at the end of 1525, "now that they have driven away the courtesans."

But neither Clement VII nor his three successors took effective action to check prostitution in Rome, although all Europe now angrily demanded reform, and there was no longer the large body of the higher type of courtesans, friends of prelates and nobles, to impede it. Rome remained until 1555, in spite of disasters, syphilis, and the rapid spread of Protestantism, thoroughly immoral. It was Paul IV, a genuine and savage puritan (though a heavy drinker, a glutton, and a man of ferocious temper and manners) who in 1558 began the reform. His statutes show a remarkable state of things. It appears that young men, noble and plebeian, are wont to carouse in the brothels, then to break the windows and throw, in the curious official language (and atrocious Latin) of the statute, "ordure or horns" at the houses. Instead of approving this, the puritan Pope says that the men, if they are of the working class, "must be fiercely tortured," flogged, branded on the forehead, and exiled; if they are young aristocrats, a taste of torture and prison will suffice. For the rape of a prostitute the Pope enjoins the loss of a hand and exile. Obviously prostitutes were still very numerous and protected by Papal law, and the treasury still taxed them. Rodocanachi says that by 1560 numbers of the more elegant were back, some making $50,000 a year, entertaining prelates as flagrantly as ever. It is the Papal tax which leads to estimates of the number. A thousand were still on the register at the end of the sixteenth century, but Cardinal Rusticucci, the Pope's Vicar, estimated that there were in all between fifteen and sixteen thousand prostitutes in Rome. Just figure out what this means. In ancient Rome, in the days of the wicked Martial, there had been 32,000 prostitutes to a million people, or about one to every eight mature males: in a city like modern London, in a materialistic age, there are said to be about 20,000 to 8,000,000 people, or one to a hundred mature males: but in Papal Rome, eighty years after the Reformation broke out, fifty years after the purification of the Church is supposed to have begun in earnest, there were as many prostitutes as mature males. I doubt if you will find that in the history of civilization except in the Rome which, historians will tell you, was now quite purified by a Counter-Reformation. Nor do I remember any other head of a religion who, when a reformer forbade girls of seven to sell flowers on the streets (often the first step to prostitution), quashed the decree, as the zealous Pope Pius IV did: or one who, like Pius V, found it necessary to forbid the nuns of Rome to have male watch-dogs. But we have passed the period of the Renaissance and will return to Rome later.

It would be as logical to say that the classical Renaissance led to the superb efflorescence of Roman art, of which Catholics are so proud, as to say that it led to this sexual freedom. The great majority even of the priests and nobles, to say nothing of the officials, soldiers, traders, and workers, who supported the prostitutes of Rome, knew nothing of Greek and Roman literature. It was the accumulation of wealth that had led to a rich development of prostitution in French, German, and north-Italian cities before more than a handful of scholars read the classical literature, and it was the same accumulation of wealth at Rome from the fifteenth century onward that led to the remarkable sexual development as well as to the artistic splendor. There is only one difference, and it is ironic: the wealth which paid for "vice" in Rome was overwhelmingly Church money, passing from the Papal treasury, the cardinals, the prelates and abbots to the tens of thousands of clerks, lawyers, shopkeepers, soldiers, and workers. It remains only to see what influence the Renaissance had on prostitution in other countries. But, as·all probably know, the Renaissance did not materially affect the life of Spain, France, and England until the second half of the sixteenth century, and that is just the period when, in each of those countries, the monarchs issue decrees for the abolition of brothels and, as far as possible, the suppression of prostitution. I know no writer on the history of prostitution, except perhaps Sorge, who shows any historic sense or scientific spirit in his work and relates the repressive laws he quotes to the life of the time. I am trying to do this as well as to include large numbers of facts that are generally overlooked. It is therefore necessary to remind the reader that syphilis and Protestantism had spread in Germany, England, France, and Spain before the Renaissance reached those countries, but for the proper analysis of the facts we must open a new chapter.

CHAPTER X

LUTHER AND THE CAMPAIGN AGAINST PROSTITUTION

THE apologist for the Middle Ages attains his aim by entirely ignoring the mass of remarkable facts I have given in the last three chapters and the still larger mass of unpleasant facts which I have given in my Story of Human Morals and True Story of the Roman Catholic Church. The champion of Protestantism welcomes the statement of the facts. Indeed, if he were well acquainted with the kind of social history I write here, he could draft a quite impressive case. By the year 1200, he would say, the Papacy had perfected its fraudulent powers and had despotic authority over Europe; and from 1200 to 1500 there flourished in nearly all parts of Europe one of the most repulsive systems of prostitution. By 1530 the Reformation had established itself, and during the next thirty years it captured one-half of Europe and shamed the other half into some sense of its un-Christian behavior. What was the result? Well, it is an historical fact that, when Protestantism spread, the medieval system of prostitution was shattered by blow after blow. In 1546 Henry VIII abolished the brothels at London. Between 1520 and 1550 most of the public brothels of Germany were closed, and the licentious baths were generally abandoned. In 1560 the French monarch ordered the suppression of brothels and the expulsion of prostitutes. In Spain in the same period Charles I and the early Philips fought strenuously against prostitution. In 1566 even the Popes—last as usual—began a serious attack on prostitution in their city.

But the apologist, as one would expect, omits two points which an impartial scientific study must include. He in the first place does not mention that in the first half of the sixteenth century, when Protestantism was spreading, syphilis invaded Europe with terrible effect, and its horrors were particularly connected with brothels and prostitutes. He in the second place carefully omits to inquire what was in actual fact the consequence of all the campaigns against prostitution in the sixteenth century. Most writers, in fact, give for the seventeenth and eighteenth centuries little more than the long list of repressive measures and police proceedings. Some, like Sanger, fill long chapters with familiar stories of the adulteries of monarchs and nobles, and they do not reflect that this new license does not merely not belong to the history of prostitution; it is one of the reasons why kings, nobles, and bishops, finding such freedom amongst women of their own class, were willing to let zealots press coercive legislation that merely interfered with the sex-life of traders and common folk. However, I have in this chapter gathered together sufficient evidence to show that in the seventeenth and eighteenth centuries, in spite of all the new laws and moral police, prostitution was in most places as abundant as ever and in many places more abundant than ever.

Let me first emphasize the part that syphilis played in the profound change of European life. In the last decade of the fifteenth century it appeared in Spain, soon passed to Italy, and was taken from there to France by the French armies. I follow the general opinion, which is still disputed, that Spanish sailors brought it from America, and that to that time only milder forms of venereal disease had been known in Europe. However that may be, in the first quarter of the sixteenth century it spread over Europe with a virulence that we can hardly appreciate and a thoroughness that sufficiently testifies to the state of sex-morals. Monks and nuns, bishops and archbishops (Cologne, for instance), princes and states-men were infected and they suffered terribly. The crude medical science of the time was paralyzed by the appalling and mysterious ravages of the disease from end to end of Europe. It was left to barbers and bath-attendants, even shoemakers, to employ their vile practices of purging and bleeding and dosing on the mass of the people. Corpses were in some places laid out in rows in the square. A very heavy percentage died, and the streets were full of visible sufferers from the disease. One cynical humorist at Paris pub-lished a small work entitled **The Triumph of the Most High and Most Powerful Pox** (it was known as the Big Pox as distinguished from the Small Pox). At first, no doubt, men regarded it as one of the periodical plagues of which they read in their chronicles, and these generally wore themselves out in from one to three years. So the brothels, though venereal contact was soon seen to be the means of transmission, continued to spread it. At Paris and in other French towns an attempt was made to isolate sufferers. All foreigners who were infected were ordered to leave the country, and Parisian patients were to await recovery outside the walls or keep to their houses. This began in 1494, but such laws could not be enforced. Travelers took the disease to every country, and it became a proverb that "the man who sets one foot in a brothel has the other in a hospital." The public baths were also recognized as, or thought to be, centers of infection. A few recent German writers have tried to show that the epidemic was exaggerated, but the evidence is very large.

Few now will hesitate to recognize that it was this which dealt the heaviest blow at the medieval brothel-system. Rudeck minutely analyzes the records in Germany, and he shows that in the first quar-ter of the century, before Lutheranism spread, the revenue of most of the brothels fell considerably. At the most we may say that the puri-tans, who certainly now multiplied under the influence of Calvin and Luther, here and there found that the ravages of syphilis enabled them to secure the suppression of brothels which the people would have hotly resisted but for the disease. Rudeck finds only one clear case of the closing of a brothel under the new religious influence. The public brothels were like the churches of Russia in recent years: they were emptied, or half-emptied, before they were closed or converted into hospitals for venereal disease. Yet in spite of the persistence of the disease, the puritans had to sustain a long and fierce struggle against people and prostitutes in every land, and in the end they succeeded only in changing the form of the system. In all works on prostitution you will find a long series of drastic laws and police actions, yet we shall now see that, apart from brief and local triumphs of Calvinism, which brought evils of their own, there was at least as much prostitution in the seventeenth and eighteenth centuries as there had been in the Middle Ages. I need not here distinguish between Protestant and Catholic countries be-cause both are supposed to have been reformed.

Let us begin with France. We saw what the situation was when syphilis arrived, the king himself being one of the bearers of it from Italy. Dulaure says in his **History of Paris** that prostitution had been "the triumphant queen of the fifteenth century," since it was "authorized by kings and favored by the majority of the celibate clergy and monks and the license of magistrates and scholars." There were six thousand prostitutes of what the Italians called the decent kind, and the preachers thundered that there were thousands of others in "every street of Paris, every vineyard, every house and field." The preacher Menot complained that mothers forced their daughters to "earn their bread in the sweat of their bodies," as he bluntly says. We have a number of these sermons, of unprintable language. The preachers represent the priests, as a body, as totally corrupt. One, preaching before the queen in the palace, said: "The goddess Venus alone reigns at your court." Sabatier finds the names of aristocratic women among the registered prostitutes: a situation which, in the case of ancient Rome (though the one woman who registered there is not known to have prostituted herself), is recorded with horror by every moralist, while the parallel case in Catholic France is never mentioned.

So France remained under its very free-living kings, Francis I and Henry II, or from 1515 to 1559, and we need take no account of a few attempts to check unlicensed and wandering prostitutes. But a boy of ten, Charles IX, now succeeded to the throne, and the Chancellor of the kingdom, Michel de l'Hopital, a puritan, induced him to sign a decree in 1560 expelling all prostitutes from Paris. We may agree with Dufour that a fairly large body of puritans, sitting under both Protestant and Catholic preachers and disgusted at the long and complete corruption of the court, had arisen at Paris; and we will not forget that the ravages of syphilis gave them a valuable text. But the fact is that Paris made a fight for its brothels which lasted five years. The brothel-owners contested the new decree in the courts; the city was full of passionate or gay and cynical pamphlets and poems on the battle. "Complaints" appeared both in the name of the courtesans and of married people that the chief means of preserving virtue was being suppressed. The law could not be carried out until 1566, when all prostitutes were ordered to leave Paris; and some other cities tried to enforce the law. If the prostitutes returned, they were to be flogged, branded and imprisoned. One can imagine what Paris would make of such a struggle.

Dufour, who has no sympathy with prostitution, says that the effects of the suppression were "scandalous," and the sustained license of the court made a mockery of the law. It is the common observation of historians that Catherine de' Medici, widow of Henry II and now real ruler of France, had a training in sensual indulgence included in the education of her sons, so that they would not care to dispute her political influence, and many French historians say that she turned the ladies of the court into prostitutes to serve her political purposes. Such was the opinion at Paris, where "The Queen's Flying Squad"—the body of court ladies who bestowed their favors in her interest—was jovially discussed. Sociologists claim that she was herself a sapphist, of which I am not convinced, but certainly there was now a very widespread practice of homosexual behavior, both male and female, and Catherine's son, Henry III, exhibited his male favorites blatantly on the streets of Paris. The records show also an increase of incest and other crimes. It is usual to say that it was the connection with Italy and the influence of the Renaissance that, while certainly helping to refine France, led to greater sexual freedom. We do find some Italian practices, such as the use of leather phalli by girls and women, introduced, and the walls of the new mansions and palaces were decorated by Italian artists with paintings of a freedom hitherto unknown. But more important than this was the fact that nobles no longer lived in provincial castles but with their wives and daughters flocked to Paris and the court; and the court, says the French historian Martin, became under Catherine "a school of corruption for the daughters of the higher nobles."

But I must not occupy my space with stories of the giddy life of the aristocracy for the next century or two. The general freedom of the ladies of the court, who now became as aggressive as in the days of chivalry—curiously, this coincides perfectly with the period of Jesuit confessors—dispensed the nobles from the need of courtesans, and they were not interested in the privations of the burghers and workers. Yet it would be difficult to believe that in such an age there was a very sincere attempt to suppress prostitution. "Never at any time," says Dufour, speaking of the reign of Henry III, the age of the pious St. Bartholomew Massacre, "was France dishonored by more stains: never had its people sunk so low in the morass of decay." From king to workers there was at Paris a neurotic alternation of vice and religious enthusiasm which reminds us of certain Russian sects. Religious processions of up to ten thousand men, women and children, all nude, and sometimes headed by lightly clad priests, walked through the streets of Paris, to invoke God's blessing on the League against the Protestants. Sometimes during the night after one of these feverish days the men and women, sleepless in their state of nervous exaltation, rushed again to the streets and formed processions. Contemporaries say that these nude gatherings had the sexual consequences which one would expect. Another fact was the sustained immorality of the clergy. There still exists a Huguenot work of the year 1581, The King's Cabinet, which makes remarkable statements in this connection. Summing up the results of a series of very detailed tables and analyses, the author says there are 287,000 priests and clerical officials or men dependent on the Church in France. To these he assigns, for sex-purposes, 300,000 adult married women and nuns, 370,000 loose girls, 100,000 procurers and passive sodomists. The figures are fantastic, but the general corruption is undeniable. Finally, we must take account of the movements of the soldiers in the religious wars. The Huguenot troops were temperate, but the soldiers of the Catholic League raped

or seduced women, including the nuns, or received their voluntary
favors, everywhere.

In such an age prostitution might be driven to dark corners
but it was not likely to decrease. We have, in fact, sufficient positive evidence that, while rape, incest, sodomy and bestiality increased (so the court records show), in consequence of the abolition
of the older facilities for sexual intercourse, the prostitutes even of
Paris lingered in full strength in the poorer quarters. Paris had
now a population of 400,000—twice that of any other city in Europe
—and the absurdly inadequate police of the time could not do much
in the densely packed and squalid poorer quarters. In the small
squares in each district were stone crosses, and these became at
night notorious centers of prostitution. In 1572 the Bishop of Paris
had to remove one, as it was "so deeply stained with vice." Paris
took these things lightly. There was a large gilt cross near one of
the old brothels and, as it served for a landmark, it was called by
everybody the maquereau (procurer). A contemporary assures us
that in 1575 there were as many prostitutes as ever, and crowds of
them followed the Catholic armies. The Chancellor still raged, and
the police at times flogged or branded some of the girls, but many
serious men were disgusted with the results, and the extreme license
of the court made a mockery of it all. Henry IV was more robust
and unrestrained than Henry III. Men told—so the contemporary
L'Estoile says—how these kings would have naked prostitutes serve
at their banquets, and in the drunken orgies at the close they would,
after intercourse, sometimes singe the pubic hair of the women with
candles. One dinner is described which recalls the chestnut dance
in the Vatican, the only difference being that cherries were used
instead of chestnuts, and there was not the extraordinary closing
scene which the Pope and his cardinal-son and daughter had devised.

In short, the character of the system was changed, but all the
French historians assure us that prostitution was as abundant as
ever. It was at this period that Mathurin Regnier, "the poet of
prostitution," lived, and the Paris depicted in his poems swarms
with prostitutes. More rigorous laws were passed in 1635: procurers were condemned to the galleys for life, the girls were to be
flogged, shaved and exiled. But these laws were generally pressed
only if revenge or a corrupt commission was sought. Louis XIV
naturally interested himself in the problem when his own period
of license was over. He provided a special prison or "hospital,"
La Salpêtrière, for arrested women. There they were given so inadequate a quantity of soup and bread that they prowled round the
garbage cans, and for economy they slept four in a bed; though the
officials hoped to avert the natural consequences of this by making
each second woman lie with her head at the first woman's feet. In
spite of a brutal whip and the use of iron collars, the miserable
women often rebelled and, as is done in American jails, filled the
quarters with their collective howls. It was a world more alien
from ours than that of the Greeks and Romans. The puritan movement of the Jansenists spread over Paris, and wandering prostitutes
were frequently arrested and flogged or lost their hair. Yet nobles

and clergy were as corrupt as ever and hundreds of known elegant courtesans lived in the city. Marion de l'Orme and Ninon de l'Enclos are often quoted as the highest representatives of this class and comparable to the courtesans of Athens or medieval Rome, but Ninon, a lady of good family, refused to take even presents from her lovers, and even Marion cannot properly be described as a prostitute.

After the death of Louis XIV Paris passed into the period of complete sexual relaxation which I described in the Story of Human Morals. Louis XVI tried in 1780 to check the spread of prostitution which this facilitated, and from his decrees we learn the situation. Brothels and street-walkers were everywhere, and elegantly dressed prostitutes sat at their windows and invited the men below to come. Suppression was now out of the question, and the houses were registered at the police bureau. But the head of the police was quickly corrupted by the brothel-owners. All that the police did was to make a night-raid once a month and bring in two or three hundred girls, many of them innocent. If they paid, they were set free: if not, they went to the special prison for from one to three months. Two retired medical surgeons were directed to examine the women and exact payment from them. They left the work to medical students and took the bulk of the revenue. Parent Duchatelet, who examined the records from 1724 to 1788, found that the numerous brothels were in effect licensed by the police, who did not notice them unless called to quell a disturbance, and it was the poor street-walkers who felt the hand of the law. It is agreed that by the time of the Revolution prostitutes had become extraordinarily numerous—one estimate says between thirty and forty thousand— and openly aggressive in places like the Palais Royal, and the brothels traded in girls of the age of twelve, thirteen or fourteen. The new Republic passed no law about prostitutes, and the number increased with the removal of all restriction. How Napoleon inaugurated a new system we shall see later.

Of the state of Germany during this period we have very poor information. The country was equally exhausted and demoralized by the Thirty Years War, and for the seventeenth century we can expect no satisfactory records. The later period of the war was one of sadistic savagery, and from poverty, rape, and loss of husbands an extraordinary number of women took to camp-prostitution. One Catholic army of 34,000 men had 127,000 women and camp-followers. The women were often put under military organization, with a sort of general, and cooked, made roads, etc., for the troops. After a victory . . . you can imagine. When civilization slowly returned, the French model was followed. The courts of numerous princes and dukes enjoyed a liberty that was often sordid. In one paragraph Scherr, in his history of morals in Germany, tells us that the court of Cleves "distinguished itself by excesses of immorality"; that the "debauched" wife of Duke William III was murdered at the instigations of her sister-in-law, who was "not less corrupt than she"; that Christian II of Saxony killed himself with "drink and debauch"; that at the Cassel court the Elector's wife misbehaved with the pages; that the Count of Koenigsmark was killed by the Prince of

Hanover for an affair with his wife; and that life at the palace of
Liegnitz was such that he will not soil his pages with a description
of it. Much more will be found in my **Story of Human Morals.**

In this atmosphere the cities developed once more a system of
prostitution. It will be enough to say a few words about Berlin.
Voltaire says of Frederic the Great that he refused to sign the death-
sentence passed on a man who had been convicted of bestiality, remarking that in his dominions "every man was as free in his ———
as in his conscience." In the last quarter of the eighteenth century
there were, says Sorge, a hundred tolerated brothels, with from seven
to nine girls each, at Berlin. Writers of the time speak with some
pride of a larger and more elegant establishment kept by a Frau
Schuwitzen. The house was furnished in the best taste, the women
all well educated, the clients carefully selected. Frau Schuwitzen
was received in society and had a box at the opera. Other writers
tell us that the popular avenue Unter den Linden swarmed with
prostitutes at night. It is said that in other German cities no
brothels or street-walkers were permitted, but this is certainly not
true of Hamburg and other towns where proper research has been
made. The system was recovering everywhere and the stricter folk
complained that the coming of refugees from France after the Revolution gave it a considerable impulse.

We have much more information about Vienna, where Schrank
especially has thoroughly studied the records. I have already told
how during the Middle Ages the finer courtesans from the public
brothels, with a civic trumpeter to precede them and robes that
were not calculated to conceal the grace of their forms or even the
color of their skin, were sent out to welcome visiting princes. The
last of these public brothels was destroyed by the Turks and, as
this was the time of decay of such establishments, no other was
built. But the city fathers looked with Austrian good-nature on
the crowds of independent prostitutes, and the ladies, dressed chiefly
in flowers, still led the dance of girls round the great bonfire on
Midsummer Night. At last there fell upon all this gaiety the
shadow of a Spanish ruler, the Archduke Ferdinand I, a fanatic who
had no mercy on Austrian leniency, and from 1520 to 1540 the most
drastic efforts were made, against the wish of the citizens, to suppress prostitution. Of these efforts and those of his successors I
need say no more than that they again illustrate the futility of all
such violent measures. In a civic document of the year 1671 relating to the opening of a new penitentiary we read that "immorality
has become quite general," in the streets, fields and open spaces;
and an Austrian writer describing his own country in 1686 says
that "adultery and lust are so common that it is as bad as Italy,
Rome or Venice." In fact the record from 1520, when the campaign
against vice began, to 1716, when Lady Mary Montagu professes to
find that in Vienna "every woman has two husbands," is a dreary
alternation of edifying laws and complaints of general sexual freedom. Hugel quotes a pamphlet published at Vienna by some zealous
citizen in 1714 on the prevalence of prostitution. Under the shelter
of the city walls, says the puritan author, there are large numbers

of brothels and wineshops in which every variety of vice is purveyed. The police arrested a girl occasionally on the streets and cut off her hair or put her in chains, but the system continued.

Such was Austria when, in 1740, the Empress Maria Theresa came to the throne and entered upon one of the most instructive of all campaigns against prostitution. It is admitted by all that at that date, in spite of a century and a quarter of police hostility, there were swarms of prostitutes, and they took such liberties that the archbishop had to order the closing of the churches and church-porches at sunset on week nights. The empress set up a Chastity Commission and directed it to obliterate prostitution. She reigned forty years and never relaxed in her efforts to suppress the immorality of priests and people. The easiest path to her favor was to engage in the work, and spies and informers were everywhere. The police entered houses night and day and searched them. The Prater, the great park in the suburbs, was full of informers, and they often hired girls to seduce men so that they could arrest them; as is done in Chicago today. There was a reign of terror in the city. Schrank, a critical historian, says (I, 207):

> During the reign of the Empress Maria Theresa no means were left untried, no sacrifices spared, even innocent families being publicly punished for the fault of one member, in order to suppress prostitution, but the result was that it increased all the more, and syphilis was more widespread.

It was estimated that at the close of her reign there were ten thousand prostitutes in Vienna. Her son, the Emperor Joseph, abolished the Chastity Commission, and at once the latent feeling found expression. From the nobility downward there was the greatest freedom of conduct, and the more elegant prostitutes hung strips of embroidered silk from their windows to indicate their profession. One saw girls bargaining in the open streets, the Belvedere Park, or the Prater. Refugee French abbés often shared their earnings and taught them French customs. Prostitutes were forbidden to appear at the theaters, but they openly plied their trade even at the doors of the churches and made, as people laughingly said, "a birdlime of religion." One church got the name of The Whores' Church. In 1789 we find Viennese complaining that the police allow the women to roam everywhere; that a dozen streets, as well as the theaters and the Prater, are full of them; that in the industrial suburbs "brutalized women" minister to workers and soldiers. In short, within ten years of the death of Maria Theresa it was acknowledged that Vienna had as much prostitution and general freedom as Paris or London. Even Austrian writers said that "libertinage is extraordinarily extensive." The police continued to find victims, but so the situation remained during the nineteenth century.

The rule of the Puritans in England was no more successful in making a permanent impression on morals or in doing more than check for a time the expression of men's impulses. There is no need to search the chronicles under Elizabeth and James I. The

reign of Charles I, most people do not realize, was more sober, and
then came the Cromwellians who gave a man three months' imprisonment for fornication and flogged and branded bawds, and for
a second offense put them to death.   The result was the unrestricted
license of the reigns of Charles II and James II, when prostitutes
could rise to the rank of royal mistresses.   The decrees of William I,
who set out to reform London in 1689, give us the surest indications
of the situation.   He published first a letter to the bishops calling
for the suppression of "vice and immorality."   It had, the Bishop
of London admitted, no influence, and two years later the king
wrote to the judges and magistrates complaining that with their
connivance vice (drunkenness, blasphemy, bawdry, etc.) had "spread
universally."   The Puritan movement had left a body of strict middle-class men, largely in the civic offices, and these responded by
forming a Society for the Reformation of Manners.   Their reports
boast that in seven years they secured thousands of convictions and
closed five hundred disorderly houses, as brothels and houses that
let rooms to prostitutes are called in English law.   A special society
of fifty Puritans concentrated on these houses, and the constables
formed another society.   There were, in short, eight societies working for the reform of morals, and spies and informers made much
money.

Traill's Social History of England, usually a sound authority,
but here warped by puritanism, says that these efforts wrought
great and beneficent changes in the life of London by the beginning
of the eighteenth century.   I would recommend the reader to consult, if it is accessible, Malcolm's Anecdotes of the Manners and Customs of London, though the author does not willingly speak of sexual matters.   He shows that in 1703 the cloisters of St. Bartholomew's Hospital were freely used by prostitutes: that in 1718 the
Society for the Reformation of Manners prosecuted 1253 persons
for "lewd and disorderly practices" and thirty-one for keeping
"bawdy houses."   In 1720, he says, a large number of clubs like the
Hell Fire and Bold Bucks had to be attacked by royal decree; and he
explains that the Bold Bucks very emphatically meant to imitate
the animal they took as patron and have relations with any female
whatever, even their own grandmothers or sisters.   Other clubs held
their orgies expressly in the hours of divine service.   Next year, the
papers disclosed, the sordid houses of the poor in London used to
admit people of all ages and both sexes, for a payment of two cents
a night, to sleep on their floors.   In 1731 a new committee started
a campaign against the "night houses and night cellars" and closed
twenty-six.

England had now passed under the Georges, and, though the
Puritan societies forced the police to act occasionally, life was as
free as in any city of the world or of history.   Gin had become a
popular drink in London, and by the middle of the century there
were 16,000 gin-shops, with riotous scenes, in the city.   For sexual
freedom, the sale and exposure of obscene pictures and books, the-
atrical license, drunkenness, gambling, theft, and attacks on the
person in the public streets the picture of London in the eighteenth

century is as extraordinary as any in history. Sorge in his Geschichte gives some curious details, but, as he never gives references
and is often inaccurate where I can check him, I reproduce them
with reserve. By 1750, he says, there were 13,000 prostitutes in
London and 1700 brothels. He is clearly wrong in saying that
the first brothel was opened about 1750, for we have seen the societies raging against them for fifty years, but possibly he means
brothels of the more elegant French type, which openly advertised
themselves. There was, he says, a large establishment in St. James'
Street (close to the royal palace), with three houses. The first
house, Aurora, contained young girls from the age of eleven who
were in the course of training. Only elderly and impotent "gentlemen" were admitted to this. In the second house, Flora, the best
girls were kept. There were homosexual brothels, and great number of prostitutes had their own apartments. It is possible that
Sorge misunderstands the "Posture Girls" who were popular about
1760, for "Posturers" was then a popular name for certain types of
acrobats or contortionists. But anything was possible in the days
when a royal prince paid $250 for a night with Kitty Fisher, and the
Duke of Grafton, the First Lord of the Treasury, paraded his mistress before the queen. The aristocratic west end at night and the
theater district (Covent Garden and Drury Lane) presented such
scenes as had never been witnessed before in London ; and all round
these centers of light were the close-packed dark quarters and the
open fields where common drabs awaited the people, while a further
swarm captured and exploited sailors along the river. One writer
estimated that there were between forty and fifty thousand prostitutes in London in 1780. I would suggest halving the figure, and
would remind the reader that a very high proportion of the remaining women of the city were very free in their conduct. Mistresses
ought not to be included amongst prostitutes, though when they live
apart from lovers who keep them and frequently change their sup-
porters, the difference is not important; and between formal "kept
mistresses" and regular prostitutes (women who support themselves
by taking money from different men) there is a broad fringe of
women who work or are married but occasionally, and in very different degrees, earn money by prostitution. Hence one quite competent observer may count twenty thousand where another counts
thirty or forty thousand.

A concrete picture of prostitution in London about the middle
of the eighteenth century can be gathered from Casanova's Memoirs.
That unscrupulous adventurer says relatively little about prostitution in Italy and France because he found almost every young
woman whom he coveted amenable to his desires. His unexpurgated
work—it should be read in French—leaves modern writers no room
to talk about Apuleius or Martial. In London, however, Casanova
complains that he found ladies more stubborn (one must remember
his ignorance of English) and, as he could live few days without
venereal pleasure, he inquired about the professionals. There were,
he says, "select baths where a rich man sups, sleeps and bathes with
a courtesan of good taste, a species that is not rare at London";

there were "houses of prostitutes, which are very common in this city"; and there were prostitutes at the call of all the best taverns. Lord Pembroke recommended the Star Tavern. The manager attended Casanova, who appeared to be a wealthy and distinguished foreigner—he had been presented at court and had conversed familiarly with the queen—and, when he heard his wish, "called a waiter and ordered him to summon a woman for my pleasure in much the same tone as he would have ordered a bottle of champagne." One servant of the tavern kept a list of prostitutes in the vicinity and sent a boy for one. Casanova did not like her, and the manager, who remained with him, told him to send her away and call another. Twenty were summoned in succession, and all were turned down by the epicure. Lord Pembroke later apologized for not giving his friend a few names. The tavern, he said, was imposing on a foreigner. He gave him the address of several who charged twenty to thirty dollars, one sixty dollars, and they were summoned to Casanova's house and rejected. In the end he met a satisfactory lady at the theater. We shall see that, in spite of all assurances of "a revolution in moral opinions" in the last decade of the century, prostitution was just as abundant at the beginning of the nineteenth century.

It will be enough to conclude with a short account of prostitution in Spain. We saw how, although Alfonso the Wise had in the thirteenth century imposed very heavy penalties on brothel-keepers and procurers (in the code of law called Las Siete Partidas), the system developed much as in the rest of Europe. Rodriguez-Solis, the Spanish authority on the subject, says that brothels were often called "monasteries"; that nunneries were very often on the same level; and that a brothel was sometimes opened opposite the church. There can be no doubt about the genial toleration in Spain, in spite of Church and law, seeing that in 1487 Ferdinand and Isabella, the pride of Catholic Spanish history, gave their chief table-steward, by royal decree, the right to establish brothels like the one I described at Seville in a dozen other towns of the south. It was in 1511 that Montigni visited and described the beautiful "abode of love" at Seville. There was a larger and more sumptuous brothel at Malaga, and Madrid, though not yet a city of importance, was full of prostitutes and had many brothels. In this, as I said, we can detect Moorish influence, for the elegant brothels of Seville and Granada were almost certainly taken over from them. They sufficiently prove that the Moors had handled the problem with their customary refinement and intelligence.

The ravages of syphilis gave, as elsewhere, a good opportunity to the puritans, and from the middle of the sixteenth century the public brothels began to disappear. It is clear that the people warmly resisted the interference with their pleasures. For three quarters of a century we find royal decrees against prostitutes and brothels repeated every few years. Sixty years after Charles I had set out to destroy prostitution, and his successors had maintained his policy, we find Philip III forbidding the prostitutes of Madrid, who were clearly prominent and prosperous, to ride through the streets in carriages and litters and to wear fine robes and jewelry. It seems even that some cities had retained their public brothels, for in 1623 Philip IV returned to the attack on them, and his decree had to be reissued, in very emphatic form, nine years later. The only result, says Rodriguez-Solis, was that private brothels were substituted for the orderly and artistic system which the Moors had bequeathed, and that "prostitutes appeared in Madrid and the rest of Spain with alarming characters." In 1696 there had to be a conference of the mayors of all Spanish towns to discuss the situation.

It was an age of poverty and degradation, and we need not look for picturesque details. Spain's expulsion of the Jews, wanton destruction of the Moorish civilization, stupid policy in America, and monstrous enrichment of the Church had led to a pauperization of the country. The population, which had under the Moors reached thirty millions, sank to seven millions, and of those, a writer of the time says, "three millions had no shirts because they had no money to buy them." One adult in every seventeen was a cleric, a monk or a nun, and they needed no prostitutes. It was, says the Spanish historian, "an age of fanatics and hypocrites, full of vices that it hid under the cloak of religion." For a time, in the period of greatest poverty and disorder, the large numbers of women who were driven to prostitution mainly followed the armies or went overseas to the freer world of the colonies. But prostitution always increased with prosperity. In the eighteenth century Charles III tried once more to uproot it, and it took a more hypocritical form than ever. A Spanish writer of the time describes a type of woman often met on the streets of Spanish towns and nowhere else in the world. She wore a semi-conventual dress of one of the religious bodies for the laiety, but her eyes discreetly questioned every man she met on her way to church. She was a prostitute. Others passed as servants of one kind or other at the inns, which were often brothels. In the second half of the century French liberalism invaded Spain, and there was a corresponding growth of clandestine prostitution. The large number of "houses of repentance" in Spain in the eighteenth century prove of themselves that prostitutes were numerous, and the references to them in official documents confirm this. The influence of the French Revolution, which was content to require public decency and did not concern itself about prostitution as such, completed the growing freedom in Spain, and we shall see later what happened in the nineteenth century.

CHAPTER XI

THE DEVELOPMENT IN THE NINETEENTH CENTURY

THE problem of prostitution, on which a vast literature has been published during the last fifty years, is in one respect simple. In a really Christian civilization houses of prostitution should no more be tolerated than schools for the training of thieves. Hence the ingenuous system of prostitution which we found flourishing under the essentially Christian or theocratic civilization of the Middle Ages is one of the humorous pages of history. The principle on which it pretended to base itself, that it is better to provide the means of fornication than to permit the danger of adultery, is recognized in no manual of theology, unless it be that of some miserable Jesuit casuist. The plain truth is that the Church had distracted attention from the ethic of Jesus and Paul in favor of its own laws and ceremonies, and, since it permitted brothels, the laity cheerfully and quite humanly patronized them. But the Reformation brought back the mind of Europe to the Christian ethic, and the coincidence of the spread of syphilis enabled it to destroy the old brothel order. The period of what one would almost call encouragement was followed by an era of hypocrisy. It is usual to call this an era of toleration, but neither church, Protestant or Catholic, nor state (as a rule) professed to tolerate what everybody called the foulest stain on civic life. Hence the many attempts between 1550 and 1750 to clear the prostitute from the face of the earth; and the invariable license that followed when the pressure was relaxed disposed men to say that, while the Christian law was clear enough, in practice one had better close one eye to the flagrant violation of it.

With the spread of skepticism in the nineteenth century and the secularization of law one ought to expect men speedily to find a social principle in regard to prostitution. It became "the social evil" instead of the scarlet sin, and reams of paper were covered with arguments about it which pretended to look only to social interests. I am not here discussing prostitution but writing the history of it, and I will only, in order that we may follow intelligently the development during the nineteenth century, point out that until recently one half the statesmen and writers were Christians and nearly all held that moral law condemned prostitution as a particularly ugly fact, whether theology did or no, so that most of the talk about "social" interests and questions was largely insincere. This confusion of mind is reflected in the whole history of prostitution from the end of the French Revolution to our own time, and it still enfeebles most of the literature about the subject.

Let us begin with France, since the French system of regulation has been so widely adopted. All the royal decrees and police persecution during two centuries had ended in giving France the largest system of prostitution outside of Asia. It was estimated in 1762 that there were twenty thousand prostitutes at Paris, and twenty years later, but still before the Revolution, estimates ranged from thirty to forty thousand. None of the various republican governments cared to pass any law about prostitution, and, since the old royal laws were assumed to be annulled, the freedom at Paris became embarrassing. Even transparent trousers were not unknown. Under the Directorate mild efforts were made to check the general freedom, and in 1802 Napoleon insisted on the police regulation of the prostitutes, which France had adopted in 1778. The principle of the law was understood to be purely social. It invoked public decency, but, with the growth of medical science, it looked more and more to control as a means of preventing or restricting the spread of venereal disease. The Napoleonic Code was widely accepted or enforced in Europe, and thus the system of civic registration and periodical medical examination was established.

With the restoration of the throne and Church many hoped to see an attempt to abolish prostitution, but the French authorities found it impossible to make the attempt. When, in 1830, the Prefect of Police issued a very severe edict against prostitutes, there was such an outcry that it could not be enforced. The Catholic authorities could do no more than press the police to use their powers against vagrant prostitutes and to watch the "tolerated houses," as they are called in French law, or virtually licensed brothels. In 1832 there were 220 of these brothels. They could not be opened within a hundred yards of a church or fifty yards of a school, each inmate must have a separate room for intercourse, and there must be no backdoor by which religious people could slip in and out. There were in addition a large number of what one might call non-residential brothels, or tolerated houses in which prostitutes (or others) could meet men. These claimed that the police had no right of entry, and the police compelled them to have two prostitutes in residence in each, so that they could enter at will.

This system remained through all the social, political and religious vicissitudes of France in the nineteenth century, but the proportion of registered prostitutes gradually decreased. The campaign against registration which, as we shall see, began in England and spread over Europe, had not at first much effect in France. The medical authorities were until the twentieth century substantially united in pleading that venereal disease could best be fought by registration, which entailed medical examination every week, and the religious protest was not effective, as France became more and more secular. But the overwhelming majority of the prostitutes dislike the barrack life of the brothel, and the number at Paris fell from 199 in the year 1857 to 45 in the year 1904. It was the same in other French cities and over Europe generally. In France registration is voluntary (except after certain convictions) and does not involve living in a brothel, but the great majority have always refused to register. "It's only the fools that register," said a German girl to Flexner. A good deal has been written on the subject, but there seem to be three chief reasons: the wish to keep entirely apart from the police, the feeling of privacy, and the hope of making more money than could be done under the brothel-system.

Hence the numbers of registered prostitutes in France and most other countries give very poor ground for estimating the total number of prostitutes. In the eighties there were three to four thousand registered at Paris, and quite competent authorities multiply this figure by from five to ten to get the total number of prostitutes. At Bordeaux, Dr. L. Reuss estimated, there were at least 5000 non-registered or "clandestine" prostitutes and only six hundred registered; at Lyons there were 700 registered, at Marseilles, the great seaport, 3500. The brothel, in the full sense, or "back of the shop," as it was popularly called, since the front of the building was as little demonstrative (beyond its name of "The Black Cat," etc.) as a speak-easy, was, therefore still a well-known institution in France forty years ago, but it was disappearing, especially at Paris. Dr. Després, a medical authority who gives full statistics in his book, finds that in 1882 there were 1,328 licensed houses in France (128 at Paris, 80 at Marseilles, 70 at Bordeaux, 42 at Tours, and at least one in every large town), with 15,000 registered prostitutes and 41,000 unregistered (half of them at Paris). The distribution of them is shown in maps in the work of Després. But the definition of a prostitute is so vague, and it makes so much difference whether or no you include the work girl who earns a few dollars in that way, that the figures given for Paris vary enormously. Speaking of the last quarter of the last century, Maxime du Camp's estimate of 120,000 at Paris is, as Flexner says, "manifestly absurd." Lecour's figure of 60,000 also is rejected as excessive, though there is a police estimate of 50,000. The best estimates vary from 10,000 (Richard) to 30,000 (Guyot). One may reasonably conclude that there were between twenty and thirty thousand prostitutes at Paris in the last part of the century, and the law was unaltered.

During that century the French population grew less than that of any other country of Europe, so that no inference can be drawn from the fact that the estimate of the number of prostitutes was much the same at the end of the century as at the beginning. One must further take into account the growth of the use of contraceptives, which in the towns promoted free intercourse and tended to lessen the number of prostitutes. We first read of a recommendation of the use of sheaths, of fine linen, as a means of averting syphilis in an Italian medical treatise of the sixteenth century, and an English physician, Dr. Hunter, recommended them in a treatise in 1717. Before the middle of the nineteenth century they were taken up by industrial production, and they became widely known as a means of preventing conception. But I will in the last chapter make a few reflections on the various developments that have to be taken into account in connection with prostitution.

The history of prostitution in England is less straightforward than in the case of France. In spite of what some historians call the "moral revolution" in the last part of the eighteenth century, we have very positive evidence that prostitution was as bad as ever in London. A thoughtful London magistrate of the time, P. Colquhoun, discussed the question in his **Treatise on the Police of the Metropolis** (1800). We actually find this careful observer, who was in close touch with the police, saying that "the unrestrained license given to males and females, in the Walks of Prostitutes, was not known in former times at places of public resort." Most writers on the subject, however, are misleading when they say that Colquhoun gives 50,000 as the police estimate of the number of prostitutes in London. He says that there were 25,000 regular prostitutes and 25,000 loose women who occasionally prostituted themselves. In the first category he counts 2000 educated women (the kind who haunted the gay gardens of Vauxhall and Ranelagh, the theaters and the best taverns), 3000 more above the rank of servants, and at least 20,000 of the rank of totally uneducated servants or workers. London then had a population of about a million, and it included 40,000 sailors and dock-workers and 150,000 apprentices. There were, he says, 5000 beer and gin shops of the loosest and lowest type. Against this turbulent and largely squalid life of London the Society for the Suppression of Vice waged a pathetic war, for the police was absurdly inadequate, and whole quarters of the city, with their unlit and very narrow and tortuous streets and courts, were inaccessible at night. The prosecutions they effected brought to light such facts as that men hawked obscene books and pictures at the doors of boarding schools for girls, and that rape and sodomy were exceedingly common. Taverns and coffee-houses in the main street of London were used for sodomy.

I have elsewhere painted this picture of London life three centuries after Luther and pointed out its significance, and I have shown that by 1825 there was no improvement. The great mass of the people, as reported in parliamentary blue-books, recognized no law of chastity and no disgrace in bastardy, so little stigma attached to prostitution. In 1837 a real police force was created, and, apart from some growth of puritanism, one is not surprised to find that an attack was made on a system which was largely sordid and very conducive to the spread of disease. The police of London then estimated that they had to deal with 6371 prostitutes; 895 of the more elegant type, who generally lived in brothels, 1612 well-dressed girls who walked the streets (which means only about a mile of chief streets), and 3864 drabs of the slums, ginshops and riverside (who might earn 12 cents one night and empty the pocket of a drunken sailor the next night). The precise figure, to a unit, given for these scattered birds of the night merely shows how absurd such estimates can be. There was, of course, no registration at London. Other police estimates gave London 9409 prostitutes in 1841, and 8600 in 1857. On the other hand social and medical workers, who wanted to inflame their readers to a zeal for reform (Talbot, Ryan, etc.) put the number before the middle of the century at 80,000 in London alone, with a further 2900 at Liverpool, 9409 at Dublin, 1800 at Glasgow, 700 at Manchester, and so on. French and German writers naturally preferred these large figures for England, but they are not now seriously entertained. The most serious estimate is that of the head of the London police, Sir Richard Mayne, in 1856. He assigned London 8600 regular prostitutes, or women living entirely by prostitution. It is hardly likely that this figure, based upon the reports of the police, is more than a thousand or so astray, but it must mean women living entirely by prostitution and it cannot include the drabs of the slums and the dark open spaces.

About this period, or in 1860, the mayor of the naval city Portsmouth made another of the many instructive attempts to abolish prostitution. It centered mainly on the public houses of his city, and he threatened to refuse to renew the license (to sell beer and spirits) of any that sheltered or purveyed to prostitutes. Between three and four hundred of the women, mostly pathetic and drink-sodden creatures of the lower type, were thrust on the streets, hustled together, and, led by a drum and fife band, conducted round the town. But the callous puritan was defeated, and the women soon returned to their haunts. A few years later (1864-66) the Contagious Diseases Acts were passed in the Parliament and, to the horror of the religious folk, medical examination was enforced in eight military and naval towns of England. On the order of a local magistrate the police could compel any woman who was known to them as a prostitute to go to the hospital to be examined and to remain there if she suffered from venereal disease. The system lasted twenty years, though ten thousand petitions for the abolition of it were presented to Parliament, one petition having two million signatures. The leader of the opposition, Josephine Butler, was the wife of a cleric, the kind of fanatically religious woman who would see in such matters nothing but a sanction of sin. But the movement for equality of the sexes had now begun, and its leaders saw in the Acts a discrimination against their own sex. A Select Committee was appointed by Parliament, and the majority of its members found in favor of the Acts. In 1865, however, W. T. Stead, a powerful journalist, wrote in a London paper, the **Pall Mall Gazette**, a series of sensational articles on the White Slave Traffic, and in the following year the opposition was strong enough to get the Acts annulled. Thus England returned to its old law. Prostitution is not an offense, but the medieval religious element remains in the sense that incitement to fornication is an offense, so solicitation on the streets and the keeping of disorderly houses are punished. We shall see later how it works.

For the remaining fifteen years of the century we shall find contradictory and often fantastic figures. Some European and American writers actually gave London 300,000 prostitutes, while one French writer and observer, F. Remo, declared London "one of the most moral capitals in Europe." Some writers assume that the growth of a puritan movement, amongst the middle-class from the influence of the Agnostic leaders and amongst the people from the Nonconformist churches, really brought down the number of prostitutes from the figure of 30,000 to a million people early in the century to some 10,000 to five million people. On the other hand, men like Sir Walter Besant, who were very close students of London life from 1880 to 1890, declared that at that time prostitution was enormously more abundant than thirty years later. The most careful study I find refers to the city of Liverpool in 1874. The medical author, Dr. Lowndes, says that the police knew of 458 brothels, 55 houses loosely used for the same purpose, and 1256 prostitutes. There were three streets of "black men's brothels," serving colored men from the ships. He concluded that there were probably two thousand regular prostitutes in Liverpool, and it had not at that time one-tenth the population of London. I am inclined to believe that something like 20,000 has remained, through all the increase of population, the sum of regular prostitutes at London, and therefore the proportion to adult males decreased tenfold in the nineteenth century. The explanation of this and the life of the prostitutes we may consider in the last chapter.

For the various provinces of Germany, which did not form a

unified empire until 1871, a few facts must suffice. Prussia had in 1700 undertaken the control and medical examination of brothels. The great growth of the army led to an increase of prostitution, and in 1792 there were 311 public brothels at Berlin, while even German travelers like Forster said that "all the women were corrupt." In that year the law was made more severe. Girls must present themselves to the police for registration before entering brothels, heavy penalties were laid on procurers, painted faces, gaudy dresses and solicitation on the streets were forbidden. The result was, of course, a rapid growth of clandestine prostitution. By 1809 the number of tolerated brothels had fallen from 311 to 200, but the city swarmed with prostitutes. In the forties there was a spirited agitation for the suppression of the brothels, and in 1845 they were all closed by royal order. The prostitutes spread over the city, and the new scandal gave so much offense that in 1851 the king restored the system of toleration and registration. By that time, as I showed in the **Story of Human Morals**, Berlin had begun to develop its remarkable night-life. Cafés and dance halls were filled with prostitutes, and some were even reserved for male prostitutes. Reuss shows that by 1870 there were 1600 registered prostitutes, and the number rose to 3598 in 1885. As in France, however, the women disliked registration, and there was so heavy a growth of non-registered prostitutes that in the eighties the police had to make about 12,000 arrests a year. They reported that they had, in this connection, to watch 2000 apartments, 800 beershops, and 232 dance-halls, cafés, theaters, etc. The German Empire had now been industrialized, and the wealth and population of Berlin increased rapidly; and, as there were several provinces in which girls had always been permitted the greatest freedom before marriage, large numbers from these rural provinces were attracted to the gay life of Berlin. Flexner, who is careful, thinks that an estimate of 20,000 to 25,000 for Berlin in 1890 is reasonable, and an estimate of 330,000 for the whole of Germany "not unreasonable." Dufour claims that there were then 50,000 at Berlin, and some claim 1,500,000 for the whole of Germany.

Berlin was, in short, rapidly attaining the position of the freest city in Europe in regard to sex, as we shall see later, and the other German cities were, in proportion to population, not far behind it. In Frankfort, Bremen and Hamburg whole streets were abandoned to brothels, and they were very numerous in Cologne, Kiel, Dortmund, Mannheim, Lubeck and Nuremberg, and in university towns like Freiburg and Leipzig. Whether the city was Catholic or Protestant made not the least difference. The old German freedom had revived, and it was clothed in a modern dress. At Hamburg, as at Portsmouth in England, a puritan mayor abolished the brothels, which were registered and taxed, and the effect was as experience had invariably shown. By 1848 there were again a hundred tolerated brothels with five hundred registered prostitutes in Hamburg. Besides these and the unregistered but regular prostitutes there were so many part-time prostitutes that of 226 who were arrested on the streets in one month by the Hamburg police 98 were working girls (mainly laundresses).

Sorge observes that we must expect very little prostitution in Spain because all the young men, and most of the married men, have lovers. I fancy that there was just as much free love in the days of the Moors, yet Spain then had the largest and most elegant brothels in Europe. There is, in fact, just as much prostitution in Spanish as in other cities, and the modern system developed steadily in the course of the nineteenth century. The French system of tolerated houses and registration was adopted at the beginning of the nineteenth century, and the kind of rulers that Spain had in that century might murder tens of thousands of rebels against church and state but they hardly encouraged puritanism. Ferdinand VII had been notorious from his youth. His fourth wife, Cristina, who succeeded him, paraded a lover before the whole of Spain. Her daughter and successor, Isabella II, was the most flagrantly immoral monarch in Europe since "the good old days," and her son, Alfonso XII, died prematurely of consumption brought on by his excesses—which conferred upon him the distinction that he was the only ruler of Spain after Napoleon who was not ignominiously expelled from the country by its people.

Under such rulers, and with a thoroughly corrupt clergy, the law against clandestine prostitutes was not likely to be enforced except when some individual puritan obtained civic power. By 1846 Madrid so swarmed with prostitutes that an attempt was made to confine them to certain quarters. It had to be renewed in 1852 and again in 1858. In the latter year the governor of Madrid made the police regulations that covered the rest of the century. He urged all prostitutes to register, as registration was voluntary, and they would then receive a card from the police and have regular medical inspection. They were forbidden to appear in the chief streets during the day or on the balconies of their houses. In 1884 there were 900 prostitutes on the register at Madrid, which then had a population of about 400,000, and there were large numbers of unregistered women. Ten years later there were five hundred recognized brothels. The situation was, in fact, the same as at Paris and Berlin, and I need not describe it further until we come to deal with the situation today.

One often reads that at least in Rome, if not all Italy, prostitution was almost crushed out of existence. What gratification any man can find in these violent suppressions, while no care is taken to pursue the action of men's impulses beneath the surface of social life in such periods, I cannot imagine. But I showed in the Story of Human Morals that prostitution flourished at Rome under the most rigorous Popes of the last century. Leo XII made the most drastic effort to reform the morals of Rome, and even Lady Blennerhasset, a Catholic historian, has to admit that only one cardinal was in favor of reform. She describes Rome as appallingly corrupt; and if we recall, as she fails to remind us, that the Cardinal Secretary of State Antonelli made a vast fortune and left an illegitimate daughter, we are not interested in pictures of the Pope setting up a telescope to see into bedrooms. I quoted every authority on the period. W. R. Thayer, in one of the chief works, says that "an occasional harrying of prostitutes, followed by the imprisonment of some and the extortion of hush money from others, seemed a joke in view of the undisturbed general profligacy." He quotes as typical of Roman sentiment the saying of a cobbler: "If I had a handsome wife I should not now be mending shoes." Bolton King, who knew Italy thoroughly, says of Rome that "on the surface it was the most moral of European cities, but in reality as corrupt as any." For the year 1860 we have the testimony of a distinguished English lawyer, Sir Edward Dicey, who knew social conditions well. He particularly studied the effect of the repressive moral legislation, which was then in its most severe application, and he declares that Rome was, "in spite of its external propriety, one of the most corrupt, debauched and demoralized of cities." Parents, he says, now prostituted their children in their own houses, and there was "a dissoluteness of the whole population." Henri Beyle (Baron de Stendhal) found Rome as easy in morals as Paris, and Edmond About wrote that "prostitution flourishes here at Rome and in all the large towns of the Papal States." I quoted the Italian historian Farini and even prelates in the same sense. Naples, "with its thin veneer of civilized luxury and its unfathomed depths of degraded life," was worse than Rome. Sodomy flourished in it.

But these facts will suffice to show how Europe passed from the period of stark hypocrisy between the Reformation and the Revolution to the semi-hypocrisy and confused mentality of modern times. The available facts as regards the United States I gave in the Story of Human Morals and will here select the few that relate strictly to prostitution. Dr. A. W. Calhoun's Social History of the American Family (Vol. II, Ch. VII) first gives a convenient text to the preacher on our modern degeneration and then gives some startling facts about sexual morals in the first half of the century. It appears that prostitutes hung round the camps at revival meetings in Kentucky and Tennessee and prospered. A southern writer having said that "in eighty years the social system of the north has developed to a point in morals only reached by that of Rome in six centuries," Dr. Calhoun, being a northerner, gives a blistering description of the morals of the south. The planters had the free use of colored girls, yet New Orleans was in such condition that a preacher of that city said that "the extent of licentiousness and prostitution here is doubtless without a parallel and probably double that of any other place in the civilized world." There were, he said, hundreds of brothels, and three-fifths of the rooms in the city were occupied by prostitutes or mistresses. The south was, Calhoun inelegantly says, "rotten to the core": the north, his rival retorted, was as bad as Rome in its worst years.

Since the gaieties of New Orleans were largely sustained by visitors who fled from the northern winter, we are prepared to find that there was not much difference, however much the moralists may exaggerate. I showed in the Story of Human Morals that there was already in the eighteenth century, and in the New England states, far more sexual freedom than is usually supposed. In the first half of the nineteenth century the growth of towns and the industrial development caused a good deal of this sexual behavior to take the form of prostitution. We read that in 1825 several brothels were destroyed by the religious townsmen in Portland, and the body of prostitutes in America must have been considerable if some sought their livelihood in towns of that small size. A French visitor to Washington in 1832, St. Victor, spoke of "terrible prostitution and debauchery," and another French observer, Abdy, pronounced in the following year that "there is a greater regard for decency at Paris." What New York was like we learn from Meade Minnegerode's The Fabulous Forties; though he quaintly speaks of the forties as "religious and prudish." Prostitutes were very numerous, and the Park Theater, where they flagrantly gathered, was popularly described as "the temple devoted to the harlot."

Fortunately we have one document of scientific value as to the state of prostitution in New York about the middle of the last century. Dr. W. W. Sanger's so-called History of Prostitution is not of much value as a history, but it includes a useful analysis of the results of a questionnaire which the author addressed to two thousand prostitutes in 1855. For the analysis of ages, previous occupations, nationality, etc.—except that I cannot resist quoting that of the 1940 who replied 960 declared themselves Protestants, 977 Catholics, and only three of no religion—I refer to Sanger's book. The total number of such women in New York Sanger estimated to be about 6000, though the police said only 5000. As we saw, there is a vague and obscure fringe to the body of prostitutes, and such estimates are precarious. But Dr. Sanger's comparison with European and other American cities is rather misleading. It is, of course, true that the New York prostitutes would be used by men from all towns within twenty miles, but it is not usual to include these in the population of a city when you calculate the percentage of prostitutes to adult males. The population of New York itself at the time was 700,000, which makes one prostitute to 28 adult males (not 40). Norfolk, the naval depot, comes next with one to 29, and many cities had one to 50. All this is very unreliable— Philadelphia claimed to have only one prostitute to 344 men—but a comparison with London may be made. Setting aside the gross figure which Sanger accepts for England and for the moment accepting the estimate, for the same year, of the head of the London police, it works out at one prostitute to seventy men. I do not accept that estimate, but it has just the same value as the police estimate in New York.

Dr. Sanger gives some interesting details about the life of the prostitutes. Those of the highest class, who were mostly of American birth, lived in Parlor Houses, or elegant apartments in good quarters, and did not go on the streets. They earned $50 or more per week, but paid heavily to the woman who lodged them, generally an ex-prostitute. The street-walkers paid from six to ten dollars a week in poorer streets. The lowest, who were generally newly-arrived immigrants, captured on the boat or at the quays, made from one to five dollars a week (and, I presume, board). They were generally exploited, perhaps at a beer saloon, by a man and his wife. Sanger made no inquiry on this point, but we may assume, on the strength of inquiries at Bremen and Hamburg, that on public holidays they would have relations with as many as twenty men in twenty-four hours. Besides all these there were houses of assignation, or hireable rooms, in quiet and respectable districts. Otherwise there was about the middle of the last century, and later, no furtiveness. Thirty years ago old men told me how they had seen the printed notice "Gentlemen Accommodated" in the front windows of houses in New York, and how in other cities they had seen queues of men waiting, chatting gaily, at the doors of the cheaper brothels.

CHAPTER XII

PROSTITUTION IN ASIA AND AFRICA

MY WORK must close with a summary survey of the condition of prostitution in our own time, as far as it is possible to make such a survey. No reader will here expect the completeness and accuracy that one could promise if it were a question, for instance, of describing the police or the clergy of the modern world. The trade of the prostitute is not included in the census and, where official estimates are published, they are apt to be enormously exaggerated or very drastically curtailed according to the aim and mood of the estimator. If expert estimates of the number of prostitutes in London today range from 10,000 to 300,000, or in New York from 15,000 to 100,000, it will not be expected that we shall find very reliable figures anywhere. There are few subjects on which prejudice is more apt to color the judgment, and even the puritan, with his unwavering disgust, may at one moment be disposed to exaggerate the number of prostitutes in his city or country, in order to inflame the anger of his followers and egg on the police, and at another moment may choose to adopt a very low figure in order to prove the efficacy of his methods and their value to the community. From the year 1900, to which I have now brought my story, until the present year there has been a world-wide campaign against prostitution. Unfortunately there are no reliable statistics that enable us to ascertain the result, besides that such campaigns are liable to have consequences outside the range of the city arc-lamps that it is difficult to estimate, and I must first collect here the more trustworthy statements I find in European and American literature and check them by my own observations in a score of countries.

In such a survey it is necessary to look beyond Europe and America, and I begin with a few words on China and Japan. What the effect has been in China of the revolutionary movements of the last ten years, or if there has been any material effect on prostitution, I have no information, but one may justly doubt if there has been more than a local disturbance here and there of a system with which Chinamen have been familiar during, probably, thousands of years. A Portuguese traveler of the sixteenth century, F. M. Pinto, has left us a description of a Chinese city as he found it nearly six hundred years ago. In one quarter of the town he found a street entirely surrendered to prostitutes of the cheaper variety, and in one of the most respectable quarters there were luxurious restaurants in which the management provided girls as ingenuously as it provided bamboo-tip tarts or bird's-egg soup or sharks' fins. The women, he says, were for the most part widows, but one suspects that this is a social fiction or a polite explanation for a European. In all probability girls were sold in infancy for the purpose, as they are today.

As is generally known, there are two chief types of brothels in China, the Blue Houses of the towns of the interior and the Flower Boats of the coast cities. It should be added that there are on the roads of the country innumerable inns at which the traveler pays for a companion for the night, just as he pays for fire and water to cook his rice, but we may confine our attention to the chief establishments. All towns, however small, have Blue Houses, or brothels with blue blinds, and often a very large lantern over the door, that sufficiently indicate their purpose to everybody. One writer on the subject calls our attention to the decency of the Chinese and says that you cannot recognize their brothels in the street. But every Chinaman knows the Blue House, which is not confined to a special quarter of the town, and, while there is certainly more decency than in parts of Europe, there is no reticence about their purpose. Every Chinese boy—girls are separated from boys about the age of seven and more carefully trained—is familiar with sex-matters from a very early age, and to the Chinese the horrified expressions of the missionaries are almost unintelligible. Parental authority over daughters and of husband over wife is—apart from the cities where the new ideas have lately spread—so rigorous that young men must avoid them, and recourse to the Blue House is considered quite natural. There are, it is true, indications of a critical attitude, as in most of the rest of the world. Officials in the public service are by old law forbidden to go to the Blue Houses, and old Chinese stories tell of girls who burst into tears when they at length learned the purpose for which they had been educated. But the law is a dead letter, and the quite general attitude is one of naturalism. When, at seven in the evening, the "Temple of Happiness" or "The Garden of Perfumed Flowers" throws back its blue-painted shutters and lights its many lamps, and the sound of song and music issues from it, men go as freely as they go to a public house in England. The doors of the cheaper houses are open to all, but there are more luxurious establishments, rich in gilt and the finest lacquer, where the more beautiful girls sit in the choicest silks, which select guests of wealth and social distinction. Even in interior towns large sums of money are paid in these, and literature, as elsewhere, abounds in plaints of the greed of the Flower Girl and the ruin of youth.

The chief peculiarity of the system, which is highly organized, is that the girls are very largely bought from their parents in infancy. The pressure of population is terrific, and one can well understand that a young couple will prefer this to infanticide. If missionaries taught birth control, in addition to giving free education and medical attendance (and often food), they would be of some service to China. In any case, we must remember that the life of the Flower House is not despised. A father, pressed by poverty, tells his own parents that he must sell one of his little daughters—I have seen a contract to sell a girl of sixteen, a virgin, for $220—and, if the grandparents do not wish to keep her, she leaves the family for life. The average price seems to be twenty or thirty dollars. The purchasers, and the collectors of exposed infants, rear the children and from the age of seven to thirteen or fifteen have them educated in the arts of the Flower Girl. For the finer type of brothel she must be well educated, to entertain cultivated men, but ordinarily she learns music (singing, the flute, and a sort of guitar) and the complex art of pleasing. She is then sold to a Blue House or a Flower Boat, and her "sisters" from neighboring houses come to welcome her and enjoy the feast. The "mother" of the community takes all the fees, for the girls are in effect slaves. The mother is tyrannical and often cruel. One reads of one who put a cat in a girl's pants and then laid a cane on the spot. The really dark feature of the system is the advance of age. The woman descends from one type of house to a poorer, until she becomes an outcast, perhaps a rag-gatherer or mender of old clothes. To get out of the system earlier a girl must persuade a lover to buy her and keep her as concubine: which may cost him eight to ten thousand dollars. No license is paid by brothels, and no tax is exacted in law, but the local rulers generally require heavy tribute.

The other type, the Flower Boat, is more familiar to American readers. It is the floating brothel of the coast and river towns. Large boats, from sixty to eighty feet long and fifteen feet broad, are anchored close to the shore and stretch in rows, connected by bridges, along it. The lowest part may be a cheap brothel, with bunks, for the workers. On the main deck there is, as in the Blue House, a large reception room, furnished in the beautiful Chinese fashion, where the girls, in loose and short silk gowns of pale rose or sky blue or golden yellow and baggy pants, sit round a large table and entertain the guests with song or story, music or reading, while the guests eat and drink. A Chinese official in Paris some years ago warmly denied that these Flower Boats are brothels. They correspond, he said, to the café-concerts of Europe and America, and the girls are entertainers like the geishas of Japan. Schultze says that formerly this was very largely the case, and other writers say that many Chinese still go, at times with their children, solely for relief from the boredom of their uneducated wives. Europeans, even ladies, are now permitted to visit them. There is, however, a general agreement that the entertainment usually ends very intimately. It is common for a score of Chinamen to hire a boat for a lively evening. The owner provides a flower girl to sit with each guest, a luxurious supper, and music. After eleven there are games and general gaiety, and the couples retire for the night to the small boats—one for each couple—which serve that purpose. Ordinarily

the boats are just public brothels of a particularly bright and entertaining character. A brave show of bunting by day and innumerable lamps by night draw attention to them, and men pay so much
an hour to be entertained. If they require a virgin companion, the
price rises very high; but virgins are easily made in China. The
membrane is stitched or otherwise manipulated, and a little eel's or
ox blood completes the illusion. Aphrodisiacs are much used, and
pictures and books of an ultra-Parisian character abound in the
brothels. Some idea of the extent of the sex-life of China may be
gathered from the fact that in the coast-city of Amoi, with a population of about 300,000, there are 3658 Blue Houses with 25,000
Flower Girls.

In the neighboring city of Chang Chu there are far less prostitutes because there sodomy is so prevalent that, Schultze says, nearly
every man indulges in it, and not secretly, and boys for the purpose
are innumerable. The practices of Chinese abroad are not neces-
sarily characteristic in this respect. They are cut off from white
women, and they are generally prevented from bringing Chinese
women. Chinese tradition is very strongly opposed to allowing a
woman to leave her native land, and the many such women in
southern Asia have for the most part been kidnapped or bought from
desperately poor parents. It is, however, true that in northern
China boy-prostitutes are extremely common. The widespread
practice is not due, as some say, to "decay," but to introduction from
the robust barbarians of the north. In Peking there are brothels of
boys, dressed as girls, from the age of eleven upward, and boys
pester the customer in the native barber shops. The Chinaman
retorts on the European critic that his moral sense, as he calls it,
seems to be perverse. In China the worst sexual offense is that
which sexologists declare, after careful inquiry, to be common to
more than ninety percent of Europeans and Americans, masturba-
tion.

As Japan was civilized from China and borrowed most of its
customs, we find there a corresponding system of public brothels of
a very elegant character. The **yoshiwara**, or love-quarter, of Tokio
has often been described. It was established in the seventeenth
century, when Tokio was made the capital of Japan and prostitutes
streamed to it in groups from all parts of the country. Since that
time millions of dollars have been spent on "the city of love," which
is now connected with Tokio by an electric street car, and it is as
unique as a temple of the goddess of love was in the old world.
Quarter of a million visitors—and foreign tourists are included—
make their way to it every month. It is a town of wooden houses,
two or three stories high, in which more than five thousand prostitutes and their attendants live. Some of the houses are furnished
with all the art and taste that Japan affords and are now electrically
lit. A grille half covers the front (like a shop window) on the
ground floor, and through this—its height indicates the amount of
the fee in each establishment—you see the little ladies in their beautiful silks and their very elaborate headdress. Upstairs are the
bedrooms and baths. The scene is even gayer than in the Chinese

Flower Boat, for the Japanese girl smiles or laughs continuously. I cannot find how many women there are in the **yoshiwara** today, for European, especially missionary, criticism has greatly disturbed the placidity of the old quarter; and Japanese officials have foolishly taken too much notice of it. At one time the Salvation Army spread the gospel of personal freedom in it, and five hundred girls fled. Later, in 1911, most of the town was burned down, and the great majority of the girls were homeless for a time. There were then seven thousand prostitutes in the **yoshiwara,** and no doubt there is something like the same number today.

The fact that five hundred girls fled when missionaries got amongst them, and whole brothels were ruined for a time because the police, under foreign pressure, said that none must be forcibly detained, reminds us that here again the girls are virtually slaves. Until 1872 they were nearly all, as in China, sold by parents for the purpose, though there was in places a custom that the girls of poor parents should earn their dowry in this way, which was considered quite honorable, or support helpless parents. In 1872, however, when the modernizing of Japan began, a law was passed that made such sales invalid, but, like all such laws, it was easily evaded. The agents of the men or firms which collected and reared children made a loan of, usually, about two hundred dollars to the parents (very largely for illegitimate or adopted children), and the child remained as a pledge until the money was repaid. If a parent ever wanted to repay it, he probably found that in some mysterious way the amount of the loan had doubled. The girl is supposed to receive half the fee, which is from ten to twenty cents in the cheaper places, but it is almost hopeless for her to try to collect her ransom. The hope of every girl is that some infatuated rich lover will some day purchase her freedom for her. Concubines are still kept in Japan, though they tend more and more to be companions for a few months or a year instead of lodging permanently in the home.

Although several towns abolished legal prostitution early in the present century, under foreign pressure, nearly every large village has its brothel, and in the cities they are numerous. Larger cities have fifty or sixty. At Nagoya, which has a population of quarter of a million, the brothels counted 60,000 visits a month or an average of 2000 a day. It used, in fact, to be the custom to set aside a day for a public procession of the more beautiful prostitutes, dressed in white silk and carrying masses of flowers. The spectacle was not only beautiful but almost as decorous as a procession of "Children of Mary" in a Catholic country, in spite of the fact that a large gilded phallus was borne in the procession. Indeed, normal behavior is so decent in Japan, and drunkenness is so rare, that the brothel never becomes the disorderly house that it does in Europe. When Professor Nitobe, a man of high ideals, was asked to join the movement for the suppression of the brothels, he replied by quoting the caustic reply of a Persian prince who was asked by a very décolleté lady to dance at a fashionable ball in London. "In my country," said the prince, "we have special girls for these purposes." Even the missionary writer on the subject, Murphy, says that in the Japanese brothel "much more modesty is displayed than at an ordinary dress ball in a foreign country." The scanty dresses, free exposure, and mauling of the prostitutes in a European licensed house would fill these dainty ladies of Japan with disgust. They entertain and eat with their guests and then retire with dignity to the upper rooms. The brothels are taxed by the government, but there is no need for the police to hover about in case of disorder. In Tokio and other cities there is regular medical inspection, and in some brothels the controller examines clients, but the Japanese, though more liable than the Chinese to contract venereal disease, are so clean in their persons that syphilis is not nearly so terrible as in America and Europe.

While the brothels increased in number from 278 (with 4555 inmates—they are, remember, small towns) to 389 (with 5102 inmates) between 1898 and 1908, they are now exposed to violent opposition and are losing ground. But this means only an increase of outside prostitution. Few readers will need to be told that the geisha, one of the unique features of Japanese life, is a very different person from the inmate of the brothel, but one finds quite contradictory opinions as to whether she is or is not a prostitute. Her profession, certainly, is simply that of entertainer; and there is no brighter in the world. The geishas are, like the prostitutes, girls who were exposed or sold in infancy and carefully trained for the work of entertaining. They are often taught science, history and literature, as well as music, and men of distinction may relax with them. At one time they were invited to public banquets, and they are often invited to private celebrations. They are both gay and refined, full of life and laughter (unlike Pierre Loti's description of one), very clever mimics of every type of Japanese society. They are very exacting or cajoling, and the moralists often warn young men against their greed. Are they to be classed as prostitutes? It is more sensible to ask what proportion of them do **not** prostitute themselves, and apparently the proportion is at least very small. Japanese law punishes fornication with a small fine, and the geishas have no license, like the inmates of a brothel. But the police are lenient, and the life of the geisha in her own room or the house of her patron rarely comes under their notice. Murphy says that the higher police officials regard them as the highest class of prostitutes. Of late years there has been a growth of "occasional houses" in which geishas meet their clients.

Besides these two classes there are tens of thousands of streetwalkers and prostitutes of the western type, especially in the large industrial towns. Murphy, a prejudiced witness in some ways, yet the best collector of statistics, calculates that they are as numerous as brothel-inmates, and they are on the increase. The police occasionally arrest them but are very tolerant. If he is right, there must be something more than 100,000 prostitutes of all classes in the kingdom of Japan, and he is probably below the mark. In his statistical table he assigns Tokio about 8000 prostitutes and geishas. Schultze, an unbiased writer, says that in 1913 there were in Tokio 6500 geishas and 6000 girls of the **yoshiwara**. If we add wandering prostitutes and those of the brothels that are kept for foreigners, it is clear that Tokio must have more than 15,000 prostitutes. Osaka, in Murphy's table, is credited with 7000 geishas and brothel-inmates; Kioto with three to four thousand. Half a dozen other cities have between two and four thousand, fourteen have between one and two thousand, and a score of large towns have between five hundred and a thousand. These tables show a total of 50,000 regular prostitutes and 30,000 geishas in the year 1896, and there has since been a considerable increase, corresponding to the growth of wealth and population. But in the last thirty years there has been, as I said, a drastic campaign against the old system, and many Japanese have been persuaded that they must remove their "shame" and adopt the "superior" system of the west. Count Okuma lent his prestige to this movement for "the emancipation of the slaves"—the American missionaries put it on a level with the abolitionist movement of the last century—and other scholars or statesmen joined. Professor Hiranuma published in 1913 an article which he entitled "The Geisha, the Ruin of the Land." There are certainly features of the Chinese and Japanese system that are unjust and must be altered, but it is a pity that the sounder and more attractive features should be sacrificed in favor of the miserable system which follows upon "reform" in Europe and America.

The Chinese and Japanese have, in their expansion over southern Asia, naturally taken their institutions with them, but the pressure of Dutch and English authorities has, as usual, brought about a loss of refinement. Singapore, with its hundred thousand Chinese, has for many decades been notorious for its Malay Street and has received recruits from China. In 1899 a magistrate's clerk of Canton was convicted and executed for having sent more than a thousand kidnapped girls and women to Malaya, and another official took up his squalid trade until he was arrested. Since then the prostitutes are, as in China, girls who have been bought and reared for the purpose. A case is recorded of a husband who sold his young wife for $30. The agent sold her for $54 to a Singapore vessel and, if she were comely, she would probably fetch $150 or $200 in Singapore, where some of the brothels are quite wealthy. Four-fifths of the Chinese girls and women who are taken out of the country are intended for prostitution, and they are found all along the Indian Ocean. It is said that there are 7000 of them in Singapore, but the figure seems to refer to the whole body of prostitutes, who are of all nations, even American, as realistic films of Singapore will have taught the reader. There are about a hundred international brothels in Malay Street, yet even European ladies, who are visiting, are taken in rickshaws along that seething avenue of prostitution and crime. The decent Chinaman remains silent and "inscrutable."

I have called India the classic land of prostitution because we found it highly organized there centuries before the beginning of the Christian Era and in the Middle Ages, and it has today a very widespread form of prostitution—temple-prostitution—which is not now found in any other country. The Mohammedans at first tried to control the prostitutes, who were, says an ancient Hindu chronicle, "so numerous in the capital that they could hardly be counted." Prince after prince drove them back into secluded quarters, they were forbidden to sing and dance, and every effort was made to convince them that their profession was shameful. It was all futile, and I quoted in an earlier chapter a fifteenth century description of a brothel system as free and refined as that of the Moors, the Chinese, and the Japanese.

Before that time, probably in the ninth and tenth centuries, the Hindu religion had taken the profession under its protection, and at least in South India temples had their hundreds of "wives of the god" or "slaves of the god" who were acknowledged to be temple prostitutes. Sir J. G. Frazer, who has collected a good deal of information about them in his **Adonis, Attis, Osiris,** says that still every important Tamil temple in southern India has its troop of such women. They are trained from infancy, and sometimes dedicated in the womb to the service of the god. In some districts the eldest daughter is always so dedicated, in others it is the rule to dedicate at least one girl. There are other districts in which a young widow or a wife who wishes to leave her husband may, even if she is of high caste, enroll in the service of the temple, and she may have her relations with any man of corresponding caste. The girls are trained for their office, and are generally, often at the age of eight, "married" to the god or to a symbolical sword. Their formal duties are to fan the statue of the god and dance ceremoniously before it, but they are public prostitutes in the same sense as the temple-women of ancient Syria and Asia Minor.

How numerous they are, and how numerous are the ordinary prostitutes of the cities, I cannot find even estimated in any work of the last thirty or forty years, but the feeling of some of the Hindu students who come to America, that they must represent their country as stricter in regard to sex than America itself, is ingenuous. At the beginning of the last century, when British influence was very restricted, there were twelve thousand temple-prostitutes in the Madras Presidency alone, and naturally, none of these were available to Europeans. I quoted in an earlier chapter the statement of a Hindu that it was the English who "brutalized" prostitution, but the phrase can mean no more than that the European introduced his fashion of entering at once upon intercourse with a prostitute without the preliminary erotic dances and perfumes and other provocative arts of the nautch girl. These things hardly refine the act, if it is in itself brutal. Naturally the presence of a large number of soldiers attracted women of the lowest castes, but at their level of life all over India sexual intercourse is no more refined than elsewhere. There is the same variety of brothels, with the same degrees of refinement and sordidness, in the Hindu cities as in others. On each side of the color-line, in fact, there is every variety of brothel, and, while a few widows or women who have lost caste may serve in the brothels for foreigners, the women are mostly Europeans (largely French and Austrian), Japanese, Thibetans, or natives of the less civilized parts of India. Some of these lower tribes, who at times initiate a girl to prostitution as solemnly and ceremoniously as to marriage, quite freely sell their daughters to procurers. You have, in short, just the same variety in India as elsewhere, and it would be curious to suggest that in a land where sex is as freely and laughingly discussed as anywhere in the world there is, in proportion to population, less prostitution.

If the Mohammedans have a repute for opposing prostitution during their early occupation of India, they certainly did not long retain the puritanical idea in their proper world. From Syria to Algeria there is almost the richest development of prostitution in the world. Cairo, Alexandria and Constantinople are today the chief Mohammedan cities, and the sex-life is more than free. The brothel quarter at Cairo, which includes scores of streets, is one of the sights of the city, and visitors of both sexes are taken there by guards from the hotels. One of the most amusing descriptions of it is by the purity-agent, W. N. Willis, who visited it as "a public duty." He was taken through street after street of two and three story houses, all packed with women of every color and race; except English and American, he says. It is, he says, far worse than Singapore. Hundreds of women yelled at him from the large open windows, at which they sit: "Come in. This house is licensed. I show you my card. O nice kind gentleman." In one window four Syrian women, two Greeks and one Sudanese pure black woman of magnificent physique sat on view, but what most disgusted the reformer was that the male owner of the brothel, a sodomist, dressed and painted as a woman and laden with jewels, sat at the window attracting clients as openly as the women. In more retired brothels one finds girls from the age of ten upward. Agents of the Egyptian procurers buy infant girls in all surrounding countries, even in Jerusalem, just as they do in China and Japan. There are also in the Egyptian towns and the whole Mohammedan world dance-rooms where a prostitute performs, an old woman beating time and a man playing some instrument, until one of the squatting spectators, fired by the belly-dance or other suggestive movements, retires with the girl. Another takes her place at the dance until all are engaged, and the establishment is then closed.

For the more expensive establishments of Egypt, Syria and north Africa the girls are trained in special colleges, and they become so expert at dancing that they can even carry a lighted lamp on the head while they gyrate. The system stretches across the whole Mohammedan world, from Syria to the Straits of Gibraltar. In north Africa there was abundant prostitution for ages before the settlement of Europeans, though there were no brothels of the customary type; and today the women mostly live in their own houses in special quarters. One recognizes them in the street by their special costume: wide pants in Oran and Algiers, long flowing robe with gold and silver belt in Constantine and Biskra, and so on. A special group are the Uled Nail girls ("white" or dusky Africans), who, like the girls of a few other towns, leave their poor country, when they become sexually mature, to earn their dowries in the towns. Most of the women here are orderly and of as grave an aspect as the Arabs who visit them. They do not solicit, but if a man looks suggestively at them may say: "Sidi, dost thou want to drink coffee?" It is a quite serious and sober business, conducted under the will of Allah. Sodomy is, however, extremely prevalent, and the women, though reluctant, have to lend themselves to the men's desires.

CHAPTER XIII

THE SITUATION TODAY

THERE is, perhaps, nothing to which the French saying, "The more it changes, the more it is the same thing," is more justly applicable than to prostitution. From the Melanesian or African primitive town to the advanced city of modern times a certain percentage of the girls and women earn their bread by prostitution. Even at the lowest levels of human life the impulse is often simply economic: the widow, for instance, ekes out a meager livelihood, the slave must earn money for the master. But most experts on the subject conclude, on the strength of scores of impartial investigations, that the economic is not the chief motive. Socialist writers, on the one hand, eager to condemn the actual economic system, and feminist writers on the other, anxious to vindicate their sex, have urged that the great majority are driven to prostitution by want. This has been repeatedly proved false. The last and most decisive disproof of it is that at Paris during the war, when (and for many years after) there was well-paid work for every pair of hands, no prostitutes abandoned their trade but large numbers were added to their body. Havelock Ellis and almost all modern experts agree that only a minority in all countries, and a small minority in most countries, adopt or persist in prostitution because they fear that they cannot otherwise earn their living. The broad human truth is that in all large social groups a high proportion of the men will inevitably seek extra-matrimonial relations, and there are always girls or women who will make a profession of catering to them. Religion may, as in ancient Syria or modern India, smile on their conduct, or it may, as in Calvinistic Switzerland, Scotland or New England, hurl its most violent epithets at them. Society may, as in medieval Europe, genially declare the women a safety-valve of irrepressible desire; it may, as in India, China and Japan, and the old Arab civilization, elevate their trade to some standard of dignity; or it may, as in most countries, hypocritically present one visage to them in the street and another in their chambers. Pressure may in one age drive them into the dark vaults of the community; naturalism may in another age make them companions of princes. But from the first establishment of towns on this globe prostitution has flourished wherever life was permitted to express itself in freedom.

We have finally to see that our age does not in any material particular differ from its predecessors during many millennia. Let me begin with a list of some of the greater cities of the modern world at the beginning of this century and of estimates taken from the best recognized authorities, of the number of prostitutes in each:

Paris	50,000 to 60,000 (?)	Prague	15,000
Vienna	30,000	Amsterdam	7,000
Cologne	7,000	Glasgow	17,000
Rome	15,000	Amoy	25,000
Brussels	3,000 (?)	Madrid	15,000
Tokio	15,000	New York	25,000
London	20,000	Chicago	5,000 (?)
Munich	8,000	Entire United States	500,000
Berlin	25,000		

The first four of these figures are taken from Flexner, a very thorough student, but one has to bear in mind that his work is rather in the nature of a tract (to favor the abolitionist movement), and the French would not admit the estimate he gives for Paris. He himself, in fact, warns us that even police estimates in this connection must be regarded with suspicion. At Geneva, for instance, which is apt to boast of its virtue, the police told him that there were only seventeen brothels and then admitted that they knew of 223 houses used for prostitution; they said that there were no prostitutes outside the brothels, yet Flexner counted forty in a few minutes on the streets. Apart from the inherent difficulty of numbering a class which is so vague and obscure at its boundaries, there are all sorts of extraneous considerations in the mind of the counter. A police official may wish to boast of the efficiency of his force and therefore give a small figure; or he may be a religious man who wants to secure the support of the churches and therefore inflames them with a very generous estimate of the amount of scandal. With these cautions we may conclude from the list that the nineteenth century, with all its prudery, with all its more respectable zeal for public decency, with all its vast improvement in police efficiency and street illumination, with all its concern about venereal disease, with all the concentration of its churches on "the social evil" because it was much safer than concentrating on brewers, rackrent landlords or exploiting industrialists, left the world, in the extent of prostitution, in much the same condition as it had always been.

It remains to see whether we can perceive any change in the volume and types of prostitution during the last thirty years. The question is of peculiar interest for many readers. One is that there has been a growth of what is called free love in all advanced countries, accompanied by the extension to practically all the community of a knowledge of contraceptives. Another cause which ought to tend to reduce prostitution is the very great expansion of the field of girl-labor and the betterment of the condition of domestic servants, who have been one of the chief classes to provide recruits. A third is that the churches, eager to distract attention from their intellectual bankruptcy by a show of social usefulness and still finding the attack on prostitution the safest line of work, have pressed the police heavily in most countries. On the other hand the growing liberality of ideas might be expected to lead to an increase of both the women and their patrons; the economic stress of the last fourteen years (in most countries) ought, if poverty is an outstanding cause, to have swollen the ranks; and the notable freedom of conduct of girls with soldiers during the war might dispose many unemployed to turn to prostitution. Unfortunately, I must here disappoint the reader. The bibliography at the end of this chapter will show how miserably inadequate is the work I have been able to consult, out of five or six literatures, for the last twenty years. Indeed, of the four substantial general works published in that period Flexner's is a special study (mainly of prostitution before 1910) for the use of a puritanical organization, the latest edition (1919) of Sanger's book is useless for any modern purpose, Sorge's fine work is vitiated by prejudice and a Socialist determination to trace everything to economic conditions, and Boiron's book is mainly a legal treatise. There may be a larger literature in America which our prudishly controlled British National Library—it has withdrawn a number of books on prostitution from its catalogue and has put large numbers of others outside general reach—refuses to purchase, but on the whole it seems that the world output of serious studies, apart from rhetorical magazine articles, of this important subject during the last thirty years has been ridiculously small. The result is that we have shoals of amateur oracles on "the social evil" and no one seems to know all the facts.

In the case of France—to follow the order of my earlier chapters—the only demonstrable change is the decay of the legally tolerated (really licensed) brothel and the increase of unregistered prostitutes. At Paris the 199 licensed brothels of the year 1857 had sunk in 1904 to 45, and I find a recent statement that of 235 houses which are known to the police in Paris only thirty are brothels of the old type, in which registered prostitutes live and present themselves in flimsy and highly colored gowns (which they may raise to their necks) to a client who is admitted by the guardian of the door. One stumbles across these places, with the external appearance of closed shops, here and there in the quieter streets or one may, if a foreigner, find a pimply and smirky guide round the Place de l' Opera anxious to show one "de sights of Paris by night." They are forbidden to invite custom, but often the woman (an exprostitute) who guards the door accosts passers-by. The girls or (generally) women form a circle round the client, he chooses one, drinks with her (on a high tariff), and, unless he has come merely to inspect (which is freely permitted if he leaves a few dollars in drinks and tips), retires to a bedroom above, the walls of which are covered with more than life-size frescoes that make those of Pompeii seem respectable. The police regard this type of brothel as doomed and, I am told, will not sanction the opening of new places.

On the other hand, the police favor the second type of tolerated (no written license is given, of course) house, which is a block of apartments technically called "a house of passage." The rooms are hired by prostitutes for their trade. The women are thus easily and very leniently watched by the police, and the client has complete privacy. There were in 1900 only 64 of these houses, with 235 prostitutes: eight years later there were 243, with 770 prostitutes. I find no later figures, but the number has probably risen considerably. The middle-class Parisian prefers this type, and the younger and more attractive type of prostitutes find it much more profitable than the old brothel, which decays from the deterioration of its women. The "house of assignation" pays well, for fees range from five francs to forty, and in some a hundred ($20, in the pre-war value of the franc), and wine is often sold at four or five times its normal price. Flexner tells of a second class establishment of this type which made a profit of 70,000 francs a year. These houses increased fourfold in the first decade of the present century. Prostitution is a semi-respectable business in French cities, and wealthy corporations own chains of houses in the best quarter of Paris. They get the most attractive girls, and these, says Flexner, "compete with one another in forcing upon the youthful customer the knowledge of unnatural and artificial forms of sexual gratification." The same change is found in all the French cities. In twenty years the 13 brothels (of the old type) of Amiens disappeared, the 34 of Havre were reduced to nine, and the 60 of Bordeaux were reduced to 16. Houses of assignation and street-walkers increased.

I find no study of the actual situation in France, as Boiron's book is not concerned with the present extent of prostitution. The chief theme of French writers in recent years is whether the entire system of registration shall or shall not be abolished. As one would expect, the opposition to it is largely, though not professedly, based upon the religious antagonism to fornication in any form, but it is clear that medical authorities themselves are now very much divided. Some question whether registration (which entails regular medical examination) checks either street-offenses or the spread of venereal disease. But with that controversy I am not properly concerned. It seems safe to say that, while the figure of 50,000 or more prostitutes in modern Paris must be regarded with grave distrust, though Flexner gives it as the best estimate, there is no reason to suppose that the total is lower than thirty years ago (at least 30,000), and there is some evidence of an increase. I have visited Paris at intervals during thirty years, and the last time I spent a week there (1925) and walked miles through the streets at night, as I do in all cities. I found the street-walkers (in spite of about 20,000 arrests a year) more numerous than ever. This was not in the poorer quarters nor on the best-lit streets, but on quiet main streets. Each girl has a room of her own in the adjoining streets, in an ordinary tenement block. French law forbids solicitation, but in these quieter main thoroughfares the police are easily seen and avoided, and one can count hundreds of prostitutes in a single long street. In this respect the situation is much the same as at London, which we will examine presently.

French law and the administration of it offer no model in definiteness and clear social principle to any other country. Strictly, the law forbids all "houses of debauch," yet the police favor the "houses of passage," which are merely a new type of brothel. The law forbids hotels to admit prostitutes, yet in a fairly large third-

class hotel on a main and quite respectable street I found amongst
the printed rules in each bedroom a clause that a guest must not
introduce a lady to pass the night with him "without permission of
the management" (without paying extra). Dozens of prostitutes
patrolled the street below. In the absence of statistics one must
judge by the general social condition. The war led to a spread of
prostitution and a general extension of free-love views at Paris
beyond what one found in any other city of the world. It was the
playground of officers on leave, in the most reckless mood, of the
vast French, British, and American armies, and was further con-
gested with an enormously swollen civic staff. Victor Marguerite's
novel **La Garconne** (of which translations are worthless, since the
most significant passages must be suppressed) showed that this war-
inebriation had led to quite a sexual recklessness in the world of
upper and middle-class girls which persisted after the war. I do
not accept at its face value Marguerite's protest that he merely
wished to help in the purification of Paris, but there was confirmation enough, in spite of patriotic anger—he was expelled from the
Academy—of the general truth of the picture. It includes everything
that you will find in Martial. This post-war audacity pervaded all
classes, and any real denunciation of prostitution in such a world is
not conceivable.

While I have in my travels always explored the aspect of the
life of the cities I visited, I naturally know most about prostitution
in England, especially London, where I have lived for forty years.
But I will condense the results of my observations and inquiries.
Let me first warn readers of German literature that in this respect
Sorge's book, which I have recommended as the best in recent literature, is here ridiculously inaccurate: an effect, I suppose, of a post-
war prejudice which is quite natural in itself but too little controlled.
He says—and he often visited London—that there is "very little"
street-prostitution, yet that there are 300,000 prostitutes in London.
Apart from the more expensive minority, he says, the prostitutes
are almost all in brothels, and in these life is particularly sordid and
brutal. There is, we are told, little free love; that men of the middle
class rarely go to brothels (which are supported by foreigners and
the workers); and that it is "very rare for girls of the lower class
to be seduced." There is in England, he adds, such a mania for deflowering virgins that (as in China—perhaps he got his notes
mixed), the membrane is sown or drawn together by astringents,
and a prostitute becomes a virgin so often that the price has dropped
from $250 to $15. London is "the greatest market in the world for
human flesh," and "child-prostitution is particularly extensive."
Child-prostitutes of from twelve to fifteen are, it seems, to be found
in large numbers round Piccadilly Circus. Sadism is very common,
but sodomy is not, because the law imposes a life-sentence for
sodomy . . . Every word of this is false, and most of it is grotesquely
false.

It is, in the first place, so far from true that nearly all the
London prostitutes live in brothels that I do not definitely know
of a single brothel in London, in the sense of a building used entirely

by prostitutes who wait there for men. There are doubtless some, but certainly not many, for the inumerable spies of the purity organizations would soon discover them, and the police, whether bribed or no, would be bound to take action. The only type of "brothel" that is common is a house of six or eight bedrooms rented by a woman who lets the rooms to street-walkers at so much per visit or per night. There are also small residential hotels, fifth-class hotels one would call them, which hire rooms in the same way. Though the London police force is one of the least corrupt in the world, there is no doubt that the men take bribes to overlook these places, for they are often in important streets. Couples do not, of course, enter them under the eye of the police, and they do not leave them together. The man generally pays about two dollars for the use of the room for half an hour (and about the same to the prostitute), so that the owner of the place can afford to pay a fine of $100 or $250 occasionally for "keeping a disorderly house." One rarely sees a case in the papers, but there are certainly hundreds of such places. Prostitution is not a crime in British law, but solicitation—which is really the old theological offense of "inciting to debauch"—and the keeping of a disorderly house are offenses.

This is the common type of lower middle-class prostitution, though numbers of the women have rooms of their own to which they stealthily take men from the streets. At the next level, in the west end and the best suburbs, the women generally have rooms of their own in lodging houses or tenement houses. There must be hundreds of them in comparatively small streets in the heart of London, and, instead of there being "very little" street-walking, I could, from ten to twelve at night, count a thousand in an hour's walk along certain routes. There is nothing in the least "brutal" about the life, though the women, as is usual but by no means universal, tend to be dishonest. The women, who pay heavily for rooms, charge anything from five dollars upward. They try as far as possible to secure regular clients and make appointments for them, but most of them have to walk the streets. A raised eyebrow, a smile, or a whispered "good evening, dear" (hardly moving the lips) indicate their trade to a stranger as they pass. If, turning round casually, the prostitute sees the man hesitate, she turns down a side street and stands to admire the contents of a shop-window. The cinemas in central London also are much used by the women for securing men, especially in the less-attended afternoon performances.

This may be called normal middle-class prostitution in or on the fringe of west-central London, and thousands of women are engaged in it. The German legend of child-prostitutes is quite absurd. There may be very secret places where children of fifteen or sixteen are kept, but the law and police are very stern about intercourse with a female under the age of consent; though the law certainly does not, as Sorge says, regard intercourse as "equivalent to a promise of marriage" and does not impose a life-sentence (but a sentence of six months to three years) for sodomy. I need not say that the "frightful excesses," of which Sorge speaks, and the

deflowering and reflowering of virgins are fairy tales. I have shown
that exact inquiries in German brothels have proved that some women
had relations with men twenty or even twenty-five times in twenty-
four hours; and we shall presently see that the same thing has been
definitely proved in cheap American brothels. It would astonish
London prostitutes, whose average is between one and two affairs
per evening.

The ordinary London police are, as a body, not keen to notice
the conduct of the prostitutes, though I have seen plain-clothes
detectives quite falsely accuse them and arrest them. But under
pressure of the churches, and by influence on religious politicians,
a force of women-police has been established in London and several
other English cities, chiefly for the purpose of intimidating prostitutes from the streets. They seem largely to be ex-prostitutes under
puritan officers, and on some of the chief routes they have in the
last ten years reduced street-walking. Naturally prostitution has
broken out in new spots. Massage and manicure places, electric-
bath houses, offices for teaching foreign languages, dancing schools,
hygienic institutes, etc., are used to attract men. But the chief
effect is to drive the women into the suburbs. I know quiet short
streets near my house where, probably without the least suspicion
on the part of the local police, several women who are clearly prostitutes live. Sometimes a pair ("sisters") rent a small house, and
they have a suspiciously large number of male friends. Nearer to
the city large numbers of them take apartments in tenement blocks
in good-class districts. Night clubs, tea-shops, cafes, etc., are now
more used than formerly. Barmaids in hotels are often prostitutes,
in the sense that they add to their income, and there has, since the
war, been a considerable growth of middle-class women taking
money for yielding to men. The court records confirm this.

In the poorer districts, about which the police trouble themselves little, there is as much prostitution as ever. Within a mile
of the bank of England there are cheap and squalid lodging houses
where a man pays quarter of a dollar a night for a bed (sometimes
less) and not much more to his partner. There are thirty or forty
beds, often ten in a large room or dormitory. There is also a very
great deal of open-air prostitution in quiet streets not far from main
roads or in dark entries or doorways; and it is not at all confined
to the poor. One woman often keeps watch for another. There is,
in fine, an immense amount of open-air prostitution in the very large
and generally unlit open spaces which are so numerous in London.
Between my house and the city there is a public open space, un-
railed and mostly unlit, of about ten square miles, and there are
a score of smaller public spaces within the radius of London. Prostitutes of the cheaper type abound on them. I have, in short, no
doubt that while the figure of 300,000 is fantastic, 30,000 is a
plausible figure, but probably 20,000 is the most reasonable figure
to entertain. When, some years ago, a Royal Commission was set
up to inquire into the matter, a witness who said that he had known
London for forty-seven years insisted that it is today "an open-air
cathedral" compared with what it used to be. He evidently had

not studied the decentralization or the poorer districts and open spaces. However, the war led to a great spread of free ideas amongst girls and young women, and prostitution does not increase because young men, and even middle-aged employers, find it less and less necessary.

For British provincial cities we have contradictory and often ridiculous figures. In 1911 the head of the Glasgow police estimated that there were 17,000 prostitutes in his city, which is probably an exaggeration. The chief of police in the rival Scottish city, Edinburgh, claimed that there were in his city in that year only 180, as a result of police activity. Citizens of Edinburgh must have smiled, for prostitutes were almost as easily found off the main street there as elsewhere; and in fact, while this official claimed to have reduced the number from 424 to 180 in ten years, the records showed that arrests had risen from 158 to 773 (in the year 1911) in that decade. Manchester also, which has a very strenuous Watch Committee, boasted that it had abolished the scandal. I found that it had become the custom there for prostitutes and their companions to engage taxis to drive them round the darker suburbs: the chauffeurs had gained what the lodging-house keepers had lost. Probably 50,000 is a fair estimate for Great Britain, but let me repeat that definite figures are misleading. Large numbers of regularly employed though poorly paid women add to their incomes by occasionally taking money for yielding to men whom they visit. I have known the wife of a professional man to exact money from men with whom she was intimate, and widows, living on "the dole," to take to their homes, in small towns, any man who would pay for a few drinks in the public house. Police estimates of numbers of prostitutes are quite misleading as indications of the social conditions.

The situation in America will be sufficiently familiar to the reader to confirm this. He will remember the Vice Commission that was set up by the churches of Chicago in 1910 and the very detailed report of its agents' findings (The Social Evil in Chicago). They found that there were 192 houses of prostitutes, 273 flats used by them, and 42 hotels which hired rooms; in all, 4525 rooms. They very modestly concluded that there were 5000 whole-time prostitutes, though they discovered 514 further houses, flats and hotels of which the police professed to know nothing, and they made no attempt to assess clandestine prostitution and did not cover the entire city. There were also lake boats, automobiles, trips to the open suburbs, misconduct in back lots and doorways, etc. An estimate of 10,000 would have been more reasonable. The knout was laid on the prostitutes and most people will know the result. They were not even effectively scattered. In 1925 I saw on the main street in the black block brothels almost next door to each other in the most brightly lit section, men pouring in and out, and colored girls in bunches at the doors loudly accosting either white or colored men who passed; and a few blocks away I saw policemen clearly in collusion with white prostitutes to trap men. I was informed that a barber would give you his card so that you could visit his "wife," and so on. No doubt there was some improvement. Documents from brothels put before the Vice Commission in 1910 showed that girls in 50 cent houses had to earn at least $25 a week; that in one case six girls averaged sixteen men a day on four consecutive days; and that one girl averaged 26 men a night. How did Herr Sorge come to miss that?

Inquiries by the Grand Jury of New York, the Federal Department of Justice and other bodies followed. When the White Slave scare proved to be exaggerated, a new phrase, "war on commercialized vice," was invented; as if brothel-life had not always been commercialized, or as if the prostitute were less exploited by the pimp or bully. However, it is quite proper that the facts should be known —see, especially, Howard B. Woolston's Prostitution in the United States and G. J. Kneeland's Commercialized Prostitution in New York City—and the more cruel or more squalid forms be suppressed. In New York City the investigators actually counted 14,926 prostitutes, or 8167 in Parlor Houses (brothels), Apartment Houses, Furnished-Room Houses, Disorderly Hotels and Massage Parlors, and 6759 on the streets. The inquiry could not be complete, and it does not profess to include occasional or clandestine prostitutes. Hence the minimum estimate for New York, 20,000, is quite inadmissible, while the figure of 100,000, given by others, is clearly a vague exaggeration. A reasonable estimate is 30,000. On the basis of this and other inquiries in 310 cities Woolston concludes that there are 100,000 women living in houses or hotels used for prostitution in the cities and large towns of the United States, or about 200,000 women in all "in the regular army of vice." Others suggest 500,000.

This was before the war. Hardly any person will question that since that time there has been a considerable growth of freer ideas about sex, and that young men now in much larger numbers have relations with girls of their own class. But how this and the continental efforts to repress prostitution, under the pressure of the churches, have affected the total no one makes a serious effort to inform us. At least, of American literature on the subject that has crossed the Atlantic or is catalogued in international yearbooks I find only a number of magazine articles which are too vague and rhetorical to help in answering the main question.

Of the state of Germany since the war we are equally badly informed. What it was from 1900 to 1914 everybody knows. Although the laws of the empire are theoretically amongst the most severe in existence—Havelock Ellis says that they penalize the householder who permits fornication in his own house—there is no uniformity in German cities, and in Berlin to 1914 there was the freest sexual life to be found in Europe. Flexner says that there were between one and two thousand male prostitutes, 30,000 patrons of them, and forty tolerated houses or restaurants used by them. Certain restaurants were practically reserved for them, and the male prostitutes very blatantly advertised themselves. They had special dance-halls, and Flexner saw 150 male couples dancing at one of their balls. He says—I leave the responsibility to him—that practically every man in Germany had had gonorrhoea, and one in five had, or had had, syphilis. Brothels, which are not recognized in law but were openly tolerated, paid dividends of 20 per cent. One was estimated to have a capital value of $200,000. It was much the same in other cities, which had to ape Berlin. The police preferred the women to live in brothels, but refused to acknowledge that they were brothels. If they arrested a vagrant prostitute, they gave her the address of a "boarding house," where "Madame" and other girl "boarders" welcomed her. It was a hard life. Seventy-five girls in a "boarding-house" at Bremen had to earn 10,000 marks a year. At Altona, where lightly clad ladies accosted you at the doors in summer, the brothel charged each woman $15 a week for board and lodging alone. At Dresden the charge was $20. Although in 1904 more than two hundred German cities reported that they had no brothels, there were such institutions of some type everywhere. At Cologne, where the number of prostitutes was estimated at 7000, the police told Flexner that there were no brothels—and then told him where he would find them. Other writers said that there was no street-walking in Cologne, but in certain streets I found it as thick as in London or Paris. At Bremen all the houses (twenty-five) in one small street were divided into flats with a prostitute and servant in each. The houses had been built as a speculation and were a failure until the police suggested this use to the owner. The value was then almost doubled. In England one of the "social" pretexts for attacking disorderly houses is that they scare away other folk and lower the value of property. Flexner shows that in Germany it has been repeatedly proved that rents rise considerably when prostitutes invade a street.

This was the situation until the war, and Sorge's book is valuable as showing how at least in one country the war has affected prostitution. The war itself, he says, led to a more widespread liberalism in sex-ideas (as elsewhere) which reduced the need of prostitution, and then came the economic depression which ruined the gay night-life of Berlin and other large cities. English and French writers generally had claimed that the particularly audacious night-life of Berlin was just one more proof of the wickedness of the German character. One could easily set aside this nonsense and perceive that it was an effect of the rapidly advancing wealth of Berlin before 1914, and the decay of the gaiety since 1918 is just as intelligible. It seems that the police themselves took advantage of the war to order all night-resorts to close, first at 3 a. m., then at 1 a. m. Night-clubs sprang up everywhere, and thus the regulations were evaded. However, the economic stringency since has completed the ruin of the famous all-night restaurants and places of entertainment. Homosexuals are still numerous, have a few obscure houses and promenade daily in or near the Tiergartenstrasse. Notorious sapphists may still be recognized in a few bars and cafés, but the wealthier women are said to distrust prostitutes, on account of blackmail, and resort to massage-establishments. The police say that there are now no brothels, but there is an increase of street-walking, and there has been, as in London, an extension over the suburbs. You pass from district to district until in poor, dark and open quarters you find the type that will, in the shade of trees or buildings, hire themselves for

a nickel. On the other hand, Sorge says, the working and lower
middle-class girls in the dance-halls are now so free that this also
threatens the trade of the prostitute. Or is it merely a modification?
A bottle of wine and an automobile ride are substituted for the
prostitute's fee.

For the rest of Germany Sorge reports a general decrease of
street-walking and gaiety in restaurants and an increase of brothels.
In the larger towns the brothels tend to keep to one street, and in
some places the civic guide-book informs the tourist where he will
find them. At Munich and Nuremberg there is little street-life, but,
proportionately to income, "as much prostitution as elsewhere."
Dresden has still a hectic night-life, numerous brothels, and plenty
of street-walkers. Generally the police try to force the women into
the "barrack system" or confine them to one street. At Essen some
humorless official chose for this purpose the Heilige Geiststrasse
(Holy Ghost Street). The weakness of this new segregation-sys-
tem is that, unless some very short street can be surrendered entirely to prostitutes, in which case the property rises rapidly in
value, the other inhabitants complain bitterly. In many cities the
police have abandoned the attempt. But everything is provisional
and abnormal in Germany at present, and we can say only that the
greater freedom of girls since the War and the Revolution has modified prostitution, but otherwise it flourishes even more than one
would expect under the terrible depression.

About prostitution in Vienna we still have more information,
from Viennese writers, than in the case of any other city. Two
works, those of Kocmata and Montane, date as late as 1925 (in
which year also I spent a week in Vienna), and Sorge is well acquainted with the city. Estimates of the number of prostitutes
before the war ran as high as 40,000 and even 50,000, but since 1906
the police had been compelled to take action against them on account
of a grave scandal. A brothel, masquerading as "Riehl's Dress-
making Salon" was found to have all the evils of white slavery.
The woman Riehl, who made a fortune, had twenty girls in a condition very like slavery, and the recruiting or decoying was scandalous. Details of age, consent of parents, etc., were forged for the
police. Employment agencies sent unemployed servants to the
place. Yet at the time of the collapse of the Austrian Empire there
were still in Vienna 551 tolerated houses, 6797 regular prostitutes,
and, some said, twenty to thirty thousand free prostitutes. From
1918 to 1922 the police waged a very lively campaign, entering hotels
at night and demanding that couples should prove that they were
married. It was found that some of the hotel-keepers were Christian Socialists, or members of the party which egged on the police.
One result was the increased of registered prostitutes, and the police
records show that a higher type of educated girl was now more
numerous. In four years there were 26,574 arrests for clandestine
prostitution, yet at the end of the campaign there were, Montane
estimated, between 15,000 and 18,000 prostitutes. The terrible im-
poverishment worked both ways: it drove Austrian girls to prostitution—one may fully admit this at a time when, the Viennese police

told me, half the workers had less than a dollar a week and the other half nothing—and the low exchange attracted hundreds of thousands of foreigners. In no city of the world have I seen such crowds of street-walkers as I saw at Vienna in 1925. One must wait for the economic recovery of the beautiful city and the fine-natured Austrian people to judge the real position of prostitution in it.

Hungary also was, like Austria, barbarously mutilated by the Allies at the Versailles Conference, and the same depression has fallen upon the love-life of Budapest, which before the war was famous. It was known as "the city of brothels," and they were better organized than anywhere else. One which was built in 1910 cost $100,000. The best of them were in Andrassy Street, where the more elegant restaurants are found. In some you found in the reception room portraits of the women, nude, from which you made your choice. You then touched an electric bell-push under the photograph and it was covered, so that the next visitor would know that the lady was engaged. The night-life was very gay, and without the morbid features of Berlin night-life. The brothels were closely controlled, the price and the prostitute's share being fixed by the police, and they had to show their accounts monthly. When a girl presented herself for brothel registration, a social worker first tried to persuade her to adopt some other occupation. If this failed, she was given the little black book—green book if she was a voluntary free prostitute—of regulations, and the police saw that she was allowed a three hours' walk daily and a free half-day every week. The depression after the war brought a severe chill upon all this, and the Communist Revolution further disturbed it by diverting women from prostitution and spreading free-love ideas amongst other girls. I found in 1925 that there was comparatively little street-walking, but the police, who are even more genial than Irish policemen in New York, were quite benevolent about the use of the hotels, even (when they saw me seek quarters in vain) recommending me to a very decent hotel in which many couples were clearly not married. But the poor Magyars and their handsome city are in too abnormal an economic position to make the present situation of interest.

I must be content with very short notices of prostitution in the rest of the world. Holland, Denmark, Norway, Sweden, Checko Slovakia, Switzerland and the city of Vienna are supposed to have the German-English system of no longer recognizing brothels; Italy (after many fluctuations), Belgium, Portugal, Spain, Rumania, Greece, Hungary and Austria (except Vienna) are said to follow the French model. But we saw how little difference there is in effect between Paris and Berlin, and all countries are in a state of confusion. So are most writers. The latest edition of Sanger says that there are no prostitutes in Mexico City, where I found three large brothel-quarters, of different tariffs, which were known to every boy of ten. Hundreds of prostitutes in the cheapest brothel street sat placidly at their doors and invited you to enter, while the "stars" from the most expensive and quite luxurious colony were as conspicuous as the finest ladies in the afternoon parade of carriages. Sorge says that it is difficult to discover a prostitute at

Madrid, and I nightly saw hundreds on the street and in the cafés within quarter of a mile of my hotel, in the year when the clerical-military dictatorship was supposed to be most severe on them. Navarro-Fernandez says that estimates of the number of prostitutes at Madrid in the early part of this century ranged from 15,000 to 30,000, and there does not seem to be any material change. For Italy we have no recent information, but before the war the number of street arrests suggested that there were 15,000 prostitutes at least in Rome; and there, and especially in Naples and the south, there was a good deal of boy-prostitution. As to Spanish America, the subject is too large for descriptive accounts here, and the last figures I have are that about 1910 there were in Buenos Aires 192 well-known brothels with 1022 inmates, and that here there is reason to speak of a White Slave Traffic (now very scanty), while experts declare that we have now no trace of it in Europe. Rio de Janeiro in 1915 had 1685 prostitutes who were regularly examined.

In northern European countries law is severe enough, but sex-ideas are so liberal that prostitution is relatively small. An exact inquiry in Sweden showed that of 582 men 464 had had sexual inter-course before they were eighteen, and Swedish writers describe the young women generally as very yielding, if not aggressive. It is much the same in Norway. There are, however, plenty of brothels in Stockholm, Gothenburg, Malmö, Christiania, Bergen and Trond-heim. Denmark is a little less free, and Copenhagen used to be called by Germans "a brothel city." In 1906, however, regulation was abolished, and the reformers professed to have abolished prosti-tution. Sorge, who knows Denmark well, says that many prosti-tutes passed to Germany, but that by 1912 the streets were full of prostitutes in the later hours. At Amsterdam, since abolition in 1911, when an incomplete census gave 7000 prostitutes, the brothels have merely become more discreet. You ask a taxi-driver to find one. In Rotterdam they are often, to the eye, cigar stores. Aboli-tion completely failed to reduce prostitution, yet Belgium followed in 1924, and the consequence was, says Dr. Marteaux of Brussels, "the invasion of our chief streets by an army of prostitutes." Brus-sels and Ostend are as well supplied as other cities. Flexner reports that when Zurich also abolished regulation, women, a high official told him, found that they could not go along the streets without in-sults. What the situation may be in Russia today, where prostitu-tion was once so abundant, it is difficult to say. Before the war prostitution was so flagrant that girls from the age of eight to thirteen used to tout at the doors of quite elegant baths, which were used as brothels. Nötzel, one of the best informed writers, says that one day, when a girl of fifteen pressed him, a rival prostitute, nine years old, said: "What do you want with that old thing?" When asked what they wanted, they would say: "You can be my father" (as the baths admitted families to bathe together). In the suburbs of Moscow were great numbers of brothels of the cheapest and most squalid type. Sorge, who has seen Moscow since the Revolution, says that poverty and free love have so reduced the prostitutes that they are confined to one street. He throws some light, by the way, on the legend that the Bolsheviks tried to make all women common property. He gives documentary evidence that at various places like Cronstadt and Saratov the local Bolsheviks did issue decrees declaring private property in women between the ages of seventeen and thirty-two abolished. The authorities were to assign them to soldiers, sailors, workers and peasants.

Since this is an historical, not a social or ethical, work, I leave the reader to draw his own conclusions, but two general facts stand out conspicuously. One is that every attempt to prevent, by law and police, women from earning money in this way has either merely driven them to change their tactics or has, when it was very drastic, driven men to the seduction of non-prostitutes. The second is that in modern times the number of prostitutes has not increased in proportion to the enormous growth of modern cities, and this seems to be due rather to the greater ease with which, largely owing to the spread of contraceptives, men find what they desire in their own class. The future of the ancient profession is far too large a subject to be discussed here, and I will merely hazard the opinion that in a few generations men will act on a strictly and purely social principle and leave prostitution to be governed, like any other form of behavior, solely by the common law of public decency. There seems to be no other way out of the confusion of law and hypocrisy in practice of most modern civilizations.

BIBLIOGRAPHY

Historical works, books of travel, general social studies and magazine articles from which facts have been collected are not included here.

Bauer, Max, Das Liebesleben in der deutschen Vergangenheit, 1924, 388 pp.

Block, Ivan, Die Prostitution, 1912, 870 pp.

Boiron, N. W., La prostitution dans l'histoire, 1926, 290 pp.

Colquhoun, P., A Treatise on the Police of the Metropolis, 1800, 655 pp.

Desprès, A., La prostitution en France, 1880, 203 pp.

Dufour, P., Histoire de la prostitution, 1851-1861, 6 vols.

Ellis, Havelock, Studies in the Psychology of Sex, (in Vol VI), 1928.

Eslava, R. G., La prostitucion en Madrid, 1900, 100 pp.

Fiaux, F. L., La police des moeurs, 1907, 2 vols.

Flexner, A., Prostitution in Europe, 1914, 455 pp.

Guyot, Y., Prostitution under the Regulation System, 1884, 348 pp.

Hale, Archdeacon W. H., Series of Precedents and Proceedings in Criminal Cases, 1847.

Harris, G., La prostitution, 1882, 200 pp.

Harris, G., Le prostitute nel secolo XIX, 1886, 201 pp.

Hügel, S., Zur Geschichte, Statistik und Regelung der Prostitution, 1865, 229 pp.

Jacob, P. L., Les courtisanes de l'ancienne Rome, 1884, 222 pp.

Kaehler, G., Beiträge zur Geschichte der Prostitution in Hamburg, 1892, 274 pp.

Kneeland, G. J., Commercialized Prostitution in New York City, 1913, 333 pp.

Kocmata, C. F., Die Prostitution in Wien, 1925, 71 pp.

Le Pileur, L., La prostitution du XIII au XVII siècle (Avignon), 1908, 164 pp.

Lowndes, F. W., Prostitution in Liverpool, 1886, 56 pp.

Malcolm, J. P., Anecdotes of the Manners and Customs of London, 1810, 2 vols.

Mammoli, T., La prostituzione, 1881, 179 pp.

Martin, H., La prostitution à Marseille, 1882, 404 pp.

Montane, H., Die Prostitution in Wien, 1925, 182 pp.

Murphy, U. G., The Social Evil in Japan, 1904, 113 pp.

Navarro-Fernandez, A., La prostitucion en la villa de Madrid, 1909, 296 pp.

Parent-Duchatelet, De la prostitution dans la ville de Paris, 1857, 2 vols.

Rabutaux, M., De la prostitution en Europe (to end 16 c.), 1881, 203 pp.

Regnault, F., L'evolution de la prostitution, 1906, 354 pp.

Remo, F., La vie galante en Angleterre, 1888, 237 pp.

Reuss, L., La prostitution, 1889, 636 pp.

Richard, La prostitution à Paris, 1890, 295 pp.

Rodocanachi, E., Courtisanes et buffons (medieval Rome), 1894,

199 pp.

Rodriguez-Solis, E., Historia de la prostitucion en España y America, 1921, 335 pp.

Rudeck, W., Geschichte der öffentlichen Sittlichkeit in Deutschland, 1897, 447 pp.

Sabatier, M., Histoire de la legislation sur les femmes publiques, 1828, 266 pp.

Sanger, W. W., The History of Prostitution, 1919, 709 pp.

Scherr, J., La société et les moeurs allemands, 1877, 472 pp.

Scherr, J., Geschichte der deutschen Frauenwelt, 1898, 2 vols.

Schlegel, Dr., Histoire de la prostitution en Chine, 1880, 28 pp.

Schrank, J., Die Prostitution in Wien, 1886, 2 vols.

Schultze, E., Die Prostitution bei den gelben Völkern, 1918, 46 pp.

Sorge, W., Geschichte der Prostitution, 1919, 476 pp.

Stead, W. T., The Maiden Tribute of Modern Babylon (in the Pall Mall Gazette, July, 1885).

Sturmer, E. L. von, Die Prostitution in den Stadten Russlands (in the Dermatologische Zeitschrift, Bd. VI, 1899).

Tammes, G., La prostituzione, 1890, 324 pp.

Taxil, Leo, La prostitution contemporaine, 1884, 508 pp.

The Social Evil in Chicago (results of Vice Commission), 1911, 399 pp.

Westermarck, E., The Origin and Development of the Moral Ideas (in Vol II), 1912.

Willis, W. N., Antichrist in Egypt, 1915, 168 pp.

Woolston, H. B., Prostitution in the United States, 1921.